JN422849

Understanding ENGLISH GRAMMAR

In Kyu Park

Shinasa

This work was conducted during the research year of Chungbuk National University in 2023.

Preface

The primary goal of this book is to help students grasp the basic principles of English grammar and establish a strong foundation for further exploration in English. Although there are many other textbooks available, I have found that they are often too voluminous to cover in a semester allotted to an introductory course. In addition, from my teaching experiences, I have felt the necessity to present a grammatical framework that meets both the practical and academic needs of those pursuing in-depth studies in English.

While writing this book, I have consulted several authoritative works that have greatly influenced my own understanding of English grammar: Quirk *et al.* 1985, Greenbaum and Nelson 2002, Nelson and Greenbaum 2016, Swan 2005, and Huddleston and Pullum 2002. Of them, Greenbaum and Nelson 2002 and Nelson and Greenbaum 2016 seemed to me to be the closest to the ideal model of a grammar textbook for college students. Accordingly, following their framework, I have tried throughout this book to explain how to systematically analyze and understand

English grammatical structures. I would like to express my gratitude to the authors of the references I have drawn upon.

I hope that this book will be a useful and accessible resource for students, guiding them through the complexities of English grammar and helping them enhance their understanding.

I would like to express my gratitude to those who have supported me throughout this project, particularly to the publisher, Shinasa, and to Ms. Geum-ran Kim for her excellent editorial expertise. Lastly, special thanks go to my wife and two sons for their constant encouragement.

In Kyu Park

Contents

Chapter 2 Word Classes

Chapter 3 Understanding the Structures of Phrases

Chapter 4 Sentence Types and Structure

Understanding English Grammar

0. Introduction

0.1 What is (English) grammar?

A sentence has its own structure or word order and is not simply a random string of words. This structure or word order can be referred to as grammar. In other words, grammar, as a subfield of linguistics (the scientific study of language), refers to the set of rules that combine words into phrases, phrases into clauses or sentences. For example, let us consider sentences in (1).

(1) a. Joan wrote an essay last semester.
    b. *Wrote Joan an essay last semester.
    c. *Joan wrote last semester an essay.

Sentence (1a) is grammatical, while (1b, c) are not grammatical because they do not comply with SVO word order in English. Grammar is not only the study of the linear word order of a sentence, as illustrated in (2):

(2) a. Julia respects John.
    b. John respects Julia.

but also the study of the hierarchical structure of a sentence, as shown in (3):

(3) a. Flying drones can be dangerous.
    b. Sylvia saw the child with a telescope.

Sentence (3a) can be interpreted as either 'It can be dangerous for you to fly drones' or 'Drones that are flying can be dangerous.' The interpretation depends on the hierarchical structure of the sequence *flying drones*. Similarly, sentence (3b) is read as 'With a telescope, Sylvia saw the child' or 'Sylvia saw the child who had a telescope.' The interpretation depends on how the prepositional phrase *with a telescope* is structurally connected to the rest of the sentence. These readings depend on structural differences, namely what the prepositional phrase *with a telescope* modifies. These examples highlight the role of grammatical structure—the arrangement of words and phrases—and its impact on meaning. Grammatical analysis focuses on how different components of a sentence are combined and how their structure influences interpretation.

0.2 Why do we study (English) grammar?

Understanding English grammar assists people in communi-cating effectively, constructing coherent sentences, and conveying their thoughts or messages accurately. It provides the foundation for proper sentence structure, clarity, and comprehension in both spoken and written English. We study grammar to grasp the nature and complex aspects of human language.

Additionally, understanding grammar is valuable in writing, as it helps people create sentences that are correct and easy to understand, making their ideas clear to others. It is important to keep in mind that how we use language can vary based on context, style, and dialect, and that English grammar rules may sometimes have exceptions or variations.

In essence, studying English grammar is fundamental to mastering the language and facilitating effective communication. This foundational knowledge also leads to a deeper, more systematic study of human language. To sum up, grammar is crucial not only for effective communication but also for gaining insights into the linguistic aspects of a language.

0.3 What are we studying in this English grammar textbook?

In this book we will deal with various grammatical items or aspects of the English language, including:

- Sentence structure: English grammar provides rules for constructing sentences, including the arrangement of subjects, verbs, complements, objects, and other elements within a sentence.
- Word classes[1]: Grammar divides words into different classes, such as nouns, verbs, adjectives, adverbs, pronouns, prepositions, conjunctions, interjections, etc. Each word class plays a specific role in constructing sentences.
- Types of phrase: Grammar divides large units (i.e., phrases) into different types, such as noun phrases, verb phrases, adjective phrases, adverb phrases, and prepositional phrases, depending on the type of head.
- Types of sentence: Grammar divides sentences into declarative, interrogative, imperative, and exclamatory sentences, each serving a specific communicative purpose.
- English usage: English grammar provides various aspects of usage,

1 This is also called **parts of speech**.

including agreement, case, verb forms, etc. in various constructions.

- Information packaging: Several principles play important roles in packaging information, such as end-focus, front-focus, end-weight, parallelism, etc.

This textbook consists of six chapters. Chapter 1 deals with seven sentence patterns, noting sentential constituents such as subject, verb, complement, object, object complement, adverbial, etc. Chapter 2 goes over word classes, and Chapter 3 examines the types and structures of phrases forming a sentence. Chapter 4 focuses on the types of sentences and clauses. Chapter 5 addresses major usage, and the last chapter covers information packaging.

Chapter 1

Exploring Simple Sentence Components

Objectives

- To understand sentence elements
- To analyze basic sentence structures
- To explore the meanings of sentence elements

Key words

subject, intransitive/linking/transitive verbs, subject complement, adverbial complement, indirect/direct object, object complement, predicate, operator, semantic roles, dynamic/action verbs, stative verbs

1.1 What is a sentence?

1.1.1 What is a sentence?

Traditionally, a sentence is the largest unit formed according to grammar, even though it is very difficult to define. *Sentence* can be defined as follows:

1. A group of words that usually contains a subject and a verb, and expresses a complete idea.[2] Sentences written in English begin with

---

2 How about these signs such as *No trespass*, *No Entrance*, *No Littering*, *Danger*, *60 kph*, etc.? They express a complete idea respectively without any subject and a verb. There are sentences composed of various ideas with a subject and a verb, such as "I confess that when first I made acquaintance with Charles Strickland I never for a moment discerned that

a capital letter and usually end with a full stop or a question mark. (Longman Dictionary of Contemporary English Online.)

2. a group of words, usually containing a verb, that expresses a thought in the form of a statement, question, instruction, or exclamation and starts with a capital letter when written. (Cambridge Dictionary Online.)

A sentence basically contains a subject and a verb.[3] The structure of a sentence can be described as follows: **Sentence = Subject + Verb + α**. The part *Verb + α* is known as *the* ***predicate***.

It consists of words as its fundamental elements or building blocks. They are classified, depending on three major characteristics,[4] into various word classes.

1.1.2 Word classes

This section takes a brief look at word classes, which will be described in detail later. The following sentence contains various word classes such as nouns, verbs (main verbs and auxiliary verbs), adjectives, adverbs, determiners, prepositions, conjunctions.

She will walk carefully across the crowded street and give a book to Rachel

---

there was in him anything out of the ordinary." (Somerset Maugham, *The Moon and Sixpence*, p. 3). Although this includes four ideas, it is normally a single sentence.

3 In imperative sentences, the subject *you* is usually implied, even though it is not mentioned directly. For example, in (*You*) *please open the window* or (*You*) *come in*, the subject is understood to be *you* but is not explicitly stated.

4 Their classification is normally based on their forms (especially suffixes), distribution, and meanings.

at the corner. (Pronoun-auxiliary-verb-adverb-preposition-determiner-adjective-noun-conjunction-verb-determiner-noun-preposition-noun-preposition-determiner-noun)

1. Nouns

A noun refers to a word which represents a person (*Rachel*), thing (*book*), place (*street*, *corner*), or concept (*happiness*). Notice the four nouns in the above sentence. *Rachel* is called a proper noun, which always begins with a capital letter, while *book*, *street*, and *corner* are common nouns.

2. Pronouns

A pronoun is a word that replaces a noun or noun phrase in a sentence, such as *she*.

3. (Main) Verbs

A verb refers to a word which expresses an action (*walk*, *give*) or state (*know*, *think*, *believe*).

4. Auxiliary verbs

An auxiliary verb, sometimes called a helping verb, is a type of verb used with a main verb to express grammatical aspects, such as tense, mood, voice, or aspect, and to provide additional meaning to a sentence. In the above sentence, an auxiliary verb *will* is used to describe a situation that is expected to take place in the future.

5. Adjectives

An adjective refers to a word which modifies or describes a noun or pronoun by giving more information about its qualities, characteristics, or attributes. In the above sentence, *crowded* is used as an adjective to modify or describe a noun.

6. Adverbs

An adverb modifies a verb (run *fast*), an adjective (*excessively* costly/dangerous), another adverb (*too* quickly), or an entire sentence or clause (*Luckily*, he wasn't hurt),[5] typically by indicating manner (*quickly*), time (*early*), place (*there*), degree (*so*, *very*), or frequency (*sometimes*). In the above sentence, *carefully* is used as an adverb to modify a verb and indicates how an action or event is performed.

7. Determiners

A determiner is a word that usually occurs at the beginning of a noun phrase and specifies the referential scope of a noun phrase, with regard to specificity, quantity, or definiteness (*a*, *the*, *this*, *several*, *all*, *some*, *etc.*).

8. Prepositions

A preposition is a word that typically comes before a noun, pronoun, or noun phrase to indicate its relationship with other elements in the sentence (*in*, *at*, *on*, *by*, *with*, *about*, *under*, *etc.*). It usually indicates location, direction, or time, and introduces a prepositional phrase. In the above sentence, *across* indicates direction (movement) and *at* indicates location.

9. Conjunctions

Lastly, a conjunction is a word that links words, phrases, or

5 The word *luckily* is called a sentence adverb.

clauses. In the above sentence, two clauses are combined by *and*.

1.2 Analysis of sentences: form and function

As mentioned in the previous chapter, a sentence has a structure or word order and consists of various constituents (i.e., units), as in the following:

(1) A brave firefighter has saved a citizen.
A B C

The sentence can normally be analyzed into three units (i.e., phrases). In the sentence, the subject (A) precedes the verb (B) followed by the object (C), which is the basic word order in English. Each phrase (A, B, C) has its own structure in the sense that any different word order pattern in each phrase is ungrammatical, as shown in **brave a firefighter*, **firefighter a brave*, **a firefighter brave*, **saved has*, **citizen a*, etc.

These three phrases can be viewed from the perspective of **form** and **function** as follows:

	Form	Function
(1A) A brave firefighter	NP (noun phrase)	subject
(1B) has saved	VP (verb phrase)	
(1C) a citizen	NP	direct object

Sentence (1) contains two NPs and one VP. (1A) is an NP which functions as the subject of the sentence, while (1C) is an NP which functions as the direct object.

1.3 Operator[6]

An operator, which is typically the first auxiliary[7] in a verb phrase, performs a specific grammatical function in forming some constructions such as questions, negatives, and reduced constructions. It also plays a significant role in emphasizing a statement.

Presented below are four important roles of the operator.

(1) Four important roles of the operator

A. In question formation, the operator is placed before the subject. This process is referred to as subject–operator inversion.

Will scientists be able to find a cure for Alzheimer's disease in the near future?
Has he finished reading the papers?
Are you ready to order?

B. The negative particle *not* is inserted after the operator in negation and it can even be contracted in informal style.

The team project *will not* (*won't*) be finished by tomorrow.
They *did not* (*didn't*) go to the BTS concert yesterday.
They *do not* (*don't*) participate in the project.

C. When the predicate is predictable from the context, only the

6 Quirk *et al.* (1985:80) define it as follows:"[T]he operator, or first auxiliary, performs an 'operational' function in relating a positive declarative structure to another major structure in the language." Greenbaum and Nelson (2016:10) define it as follows:"The operator is the first or only auxiliary verb in the verb phrase."

7 Auxiliaries are known to have NICE (**N**egation, **I**nversion, **C**ode, and **E**mphasis) properties (Palmer 1990, Aarts 2011).

operator remains, with other elements omitted.

Joan hasn't finished her assignment, but Rachel *has*.
A: Are you ready to go?
B: Yes, I *am*.
A: Can you go to the Taylor Swift concert tomorrow?
B: Yes, I *can*.

D. Stress is assigned to the operator when it is highlighted or emphasized in speech.

A: Clean your room.
B: I ***have*** cleaned it.
A: I don't like to paint the fence.
B: You ***should*** paint it.

Many sentences, on the other hand, do not have any operator (i.e., auxiliary), as shown in *Joan finished her research project yesterday*. These sentences include only the main verb. When forming certain constructions, such as questions, negatives, reduced constructions, and emphasized sentences, we use the verb *do* (*do*, *does*, *did*) called a **dummy operator** as follows:

(2) Four important roles of the dummy operator

A. Question: *Did* Joan finish her research project yesterday?
B. Negation: Joan *did not* finish her research project yesterday.
C. Reduced clause: Joan finished her research project yesterday and her best friend *did* too.
D. Emphasis: Joan *did* finish her research project yesterday.

Additionally, when a sentence includes the verb *be* (*am*, *are*, *is*) as the main verb, as in *This picture is very valuable*, the verb functions as the operator.

(3) Four important roles of the verb *be* as the operator

A. Question: *Is* this picture very valuable?
B. Negation: This picture *is not* very valuable.
C. Reduced clause: This picture is very valuable, and that one *is* too. (with the operator *is* understood)
D. Emphasis: Yes, they really ***are*** very valuable.

These operators often convey information about tense, aspect, mood, or modality. Operators, except for the verb *be*, work in conjunction with a main verb to convey additional meaning or grammatical effects. Operators lie within verb phrases. The operator is the only finite auxiliary verb, as exemplified in *He may have passed the exam.*

1.4 Essential elements of a sentence: subject and verb

A sentence describes a situation and as mentioned earlier, typically includes at least two main elements (the subject and the verb) as follows:

• Subject + Predicate (Verb + other elements)

The kid fell.
Your project is great.
I like apples.
Joan gave me a book.
They elected him mayor.
She lives in Seoul.
He put his car in the garage.

• The importance and role of the verb

The verb is the most crucial part of a sentence. Every complete sentence must contain a verb, which determines the choice of other elements such as direct objects, indirect objects, or complements, depending on its type. A verb describes an action or state, indicating what the subject is doing or what its condition is. It follows the subject in a sentence and must agree with it in number.

Sentences can usually include other constituents or elements besides the subject and the verb. In English, sentences can be divided into seven basic patterns based on their structure (i.e., word order).[8] These patterns describe the various ways in which words and phrases can be put together to form grammatically correct sentences. The choice of sentence patterns depends on the intended meaning and the main verb of the sentence.

• Basic sentence pattern

Consider the following sentences, which are composed of a subject and a verb and correspond to **Sentence Pattern I**:

8 Five sentence patterns have been used for a long time in Korea, which were originated from Onions 1904. He classified predicate forms into five patterns. In this connection, some research has presented several problems and alternative sentence patterns (Han 2008, Jung 2010, Nam 2014, Cho 2014, Hwang 2016, among others). In this textbook, the number of sentence patterns is based on Quirk *et al.* 1985. On the other hand, Hornby (1975) listed 25 verb patterns descriptively, focusing on the structure of the verb and its relationship with other elements in the sentence. This classification provides a comprehensive overview of various sentence structures. However, it seems that many of these patterns could be further narrowed down.

The wind *stilled* (soon).
The stars *are shining* (very brightly).
My cat *has disappeared* (suddenly).
He *can swim* (in the lake).
A student *has been singing* (loudly).
Joan *sneezed* (suddenly).
Sarah Brightman *sings* (beautifully).
(Luckily,) his plan *succeeded.*

In these examples, the verbs are used without any obligatory elements and are known as **intransitive verbs**. The elements in parentheses are optional, functioning as **adverbials** that provide additional context or information in the sentences. Their positions may be relatively flexible within the sentences, as shown in the following examples:

My cat has disappeared suddenly.
My cat has suddenly disappeared.
Suddenly, my cat has disappeared.

On the other hand, adverbials are different from post-modifiers (i.e., prepositional phrases) in noun phrases. An adverbial adds extra information to a clause, while a post-modifier provides more information about the noun:

They$_{S}$ have closed$_{V}$ [that restaurant *on King Street*$_{post\text{-}modifier}$]$_{DO}$.
He$_{S}$ stood$_{V}$ [*on King Street*]$_{A}$.

In the sentences above, the prepositional phrase *on King Street* functions as a post-modifier and an adverbial respectively.

• Characteristics of the subject

The subject is typically a noun phrase whose head is a noun or a pronoun. Its major characteristics include the following:

1. **Position**: The subject usually precedes the verb in declarative sentences.
2. **Pronoun forms**: Personal pronouns have specific forms when functioning as subjects (e.g., *I*, *he*, *they*: *He is reading a book*).
3. **Subject-verb agreement**: In the present tense, the subject and verb must agree in number. A singular subject takes a singular verb (e.g., *She plays the violin.*), while a plural subject takes a plural verb (e.g., *They play soccer every morning.*).
4. **Inversion in questions**: Subject-operator order in a declarative sentence is inverted in (tag) questions and certain constructions (e.g., *Are you going to the BTS concert?*). When *wh*-words function as subjects, they precede the verb (e.g., *Who broke the vase?* and *What brought you here?*).
5. **Implied subjects in imperatives**: In imperative sentences (commands or requests), the subject is often implied and understood to be the pronoun *you*[9] (e.g., *Open the window.*).
6. **Reflexive pronouns**: When two noun phrases refer to the same entity (person or thing) in the same clause, the subject determines the form of the second noun phrase (i.e., the reflexive pronoun) (e.g., *He helped himself to snacks at the party*, *The door opened by itself.*).
7. **Active-passive construction**: In a passive sentence, the subject of an active sentence becomes a prepositional phrase with *by*, while

9 How do you know that the omitted subject is *you?*

the direct object becomes the subject (e.g., *The dog chased the cat* becomes *The cat was chased by the dog.*).

• **Expanding sentence structure**

While the subject-verb structure forms the basic frame of a sentence, additional elements like objects, complements, and adverbials can be included to provide more information and detail.

1.5 Linking verbs and subject complements

Linking verbs, also known as copulas, connect the subject of a sentence to a required subject complement, which can be a noun, pronoun, or adjective that identifies, characterizes, or describes the subject. Common linking verbs include *be* (*am*, *are*, *is*, *was*, *were*, etc.)[10], *become*, *seem*, *appear*, *look*, *sound*, *feel*, *smell*, and *taste*. Here are some examples:

He *is* a physician and mathematician.
Her voice *sounded* nervous on the phone.
The soup *tastes* delicious.
She *felt* upset.

The above examples correspond to **Sentence Pattern II**.

10 The verb *be* is used not only as a linking verb (or copula) but also as a main verb meaning 'to exist.'

1.6 Transitive verbs and direct objects

A transitive verb is a type of verb that requires one or more objects to complete its meaning. For example, in the sentence *She bought a new car*, the verb *bought* is transitive because it affects the direct object *a new car*. This distinguishes transitive verbs from intransitive verbs, which do not require an object. This structure (Subject + Verb + Direct Object) corresponds to **Sentence Pattern III**.

Transitive verbs are followed by a direct object, which is the noun or noun phrase that receives the action of the verb. Without the direct object, the sentence would not make complete sense. The direct object in a sentence has several grammatical features:

1. **Position**: The direct object typically follows the verb.
2. **Pronoun forms**: Personal pronouns have specific forms when functioning as direct objects (e.g., *me*, *him*, *them*: *The supervisor praised him for his effort.*).
3. **Reflexive pronouns**: When the subject and direct object refer to the same entity (person or thing) in the same clause, the direct object takes the reflexive form[11] (e.g., *He helped himself to snacks at the party*, *She saw herself in the mirror.*).
4. **Active-passive construction**: In a passive sentence, the direct object of an active sentence becomes the subject (e.g., *The dog chased the cat* becomes *The cat was chased by the dog.*).

11 There are some exceptions, such as *The sounds that you hear around you can greatly influence your mood*, *Don't forget to bring your notebook with you*, *She brought her friends with her*, and *We need to talk about the issues between us.* (cf. *The door opened by itself.*)

1.7 Ditransitive verbs: indirect object and direct object

Some verbs, known as ditransitive verbs, require two objects: an indirect object and a direct object. While both indirect and direct objects are components of sentences typically affected by the action of the verb, they play different roles. An indirect object is a noun or pronoun that indicates to whom or for whom the action of the verb is performed. It typically functions as a recipient or beneficiary and usually appears before the direct object as follows:

Joan gave *your sister* a birthday gift.
John sent *his parents* a silver anniversary present.
They bought *their daughter* a new bicycle.
I asked *my teacher* a question.

This structure (Subject + Verb + Indirect Object + Direct Object) corresponds to **Sentence Pattern IV**.

The indirect object can be repositioned after the direct object by adding *to*, *for*, or *of* before it, depending on the verb as follows:

Joan gave a birthday gift *to your sister.*
John sent a silver anniversary present *to his parents*.
They bought a new bicycle *for their daughter*.
I asked a question *of my teacher*.

The postposed elements receive focus, aligning with the principle of end-focus, which states that the most significant information typically appears at the end of a sentence.

The indirect object in a sentence shares several grammatical features with the direct object mentioned above.

1. **Position**: The indirect object typically appears after the verb and before the direct object.

2. **Pronoun forms**: Personal pronouns have specific forms when functioning as indirect objects (e.g., *me, him, them*: *The team leader showed them the new project.*).

3. **Reflexive pronouns**: When the subject and indirect object refer to the same entity (person or thing) in the same clause, the indirect object takes the reflexive form (e.g., *Joan gave herself a break after a long day.*)

4. **Active-passive construction**: In a passive sentence, the indirect object of an active sentence can become the subject (e.g., *They have awarded Han Kang the 2024 Nobel Prize in literature* becomes *Han Kang has been awarded the 2024 Nobel Prize in literature.* When the direct object becomes the subject in a passive sentence, the preposition (*to* or *for*, depending on the verb) generally is added before the indirect object as shown in *The 2024 Nobel Prize in literature has been awarded to Han Kang.*).

1.8 Direct object and object complement

Unlike verbs requiring two objects, a certain verb requires a direct object and an object complement.

Sam painted *the wall bright blue*. (≈The wall is bright blue.)[12]

---

12 The symbol '≈' indicates 'corresponds to.'

The boss appointed *her the new manager*. (≈She is the new manager.)
They elected *her their president*. (≈She is their president.)
He considers *the movie a masterpiece*. (≈The movie is a masterpiece.)
We named *the dog Max*. (≈The dog is Max.)
I found *the homework too difficult*. (≈The assignment is too difficult.)

In these examples, the object complements provide additional information about the direct objects, completing the meanings of the sentences. This structure (Subject + Verb + Direct Object + Object Complement) corresponds to **Sentence Pattern V**. The link between a direct object and an object complement is comparable to that between a subject and a subject complement, as illustrated in the examples provided in parentheses.

1.9 Adverbial complement

As mentioned earlier, an adverbial[13] optionally modifies a verb or an entire clause. Adverbials provide additional information such as *when*, *where*, *how*, or *why something happens*. They typically correspond to the answers to questions like: *How?* (e.g., *quickly*, *carefully*), *When?* (e.g., *yesterday*, *soon*), *Where?* (e.g., *here*, *outside*), *Why?* (e.g., *because (of)…*, *owing to…*).

In contrast, an adverbial complement is necessary in order to complete the meaning of a sentence, as illustrated in the following:

13 *Adverbials* are often referred to as *adjuncts*. An adjunct is a phrase which is not necessary to the structure of the clause, but which adds some extra meaning to it.

The BTS concert lasted *for three hours.*
The trail also goes *to an old mining site.*
They are going to stay *in the guest house.*
He is *in the classroom.*
The Kamehameha Highway goes *around the entire island of Oahu.*
Machu Picchu lies *around 13 degrees south of the equator.*
A road runs *through a lush green field kissed by the sun.*
He majored *in linguistics*, a subject that fascinated him.

Verbs such as *last*, *go*, *lie*, *run*, *stay*, and so on need adverbial complements to complete the meanings of the sentences. In the sentence *He is in the classroom*, the verb *is* indicates the existence or presence of the subject, rather than simply linking it to a subject complement. In this case, the verb (*is*) is used to state that the subject (*he*) exists in the specified location (*the classroom*).

These sentences fall under **Sentence Pattern VI (SVAC)**. Adverb phrases, prepositional phrases, or clauses can function as adverbial complements, providing essential information that completes the meaning of the verb.

1.10 Direct object and adverbial complement

The direct object can be followed by an **adverbial complement.** The verb *put* must have a complement saying *where something is put*. Without the complement (*in the soup*), the sentence would not be complete as illustrated in the following:

He$_S$ put$_V$ some salt$_O$ in the soup$_{AC}$.
*He$_S$ put$_V$ some salt$_O$.

We cannot just say **He put some salt*. Here are more examples:

He put his car *in the garage*. (≈His car is in the garage.)
She kept her eyes *on the kid*. (≈Her eyes are on the kid.)
Rachel placed her hand on its head. (≈Her hand is on its head.)
Keep/Get your hands *off me*. (≈Your hands are off me.)
The curator showed us *into the National Gallery*.
(?*We are into the National Gallery, ≈We go into the National Gallery.)
He talked his son *out of it*. (≈?His son is out of it.)
This Highway takes you *to the North Shore*.
(?*You are to the North Shore, ≈You go to the North Shore.)
The doorman showed the guests into the drawing room.[14]
(?*The guests are into the drawing room.)

In the case of the first three sentences above, the relationship between the direct objects (*his car*, *her eyes*, *her hand*) and the adverbial complements (*in the garage*, *on the kid*, *on its head*) is similar to the relationship between the subjects and the adverbial complements.

However, this relationship differs from that between subjects and subject complements (which describe or identify the subject). Although the verb *be* (meaning *exist*) can be used between them (as shown in parentheses), the functional roles in the sentence structure remain distinct. The above examples show that the

14 This is from Quirk, *et al*. 1985:56. Unlike the other examples (*His car is in the garage*, *Her eyes are on the kid*), the relation between the direct object (*the guests*) and the object complement (*into the drawing room*) does not correspond to the unnatural sentence (?**The guests are into the drawing room*). Instead, it aligns more with the sentence *The guests go into the drawing room*. For your information, grammatical judgement is well known to be a matter of degree in general. Thus, *, ?*, ??, and ? usually express different degrees of ungrammaticality or unacceptability. The first symbol (*) represents fully ungrammatical or unacceptable expressions, while the last symbol (?) represents marginal expressions (Kim 2014:61).

sentences take direct object-adverbial complement structure after the verb, with adverbial complements being used obligatorily. This structure (S V DO AC) corresponds to **Sentence Pattern VII**.

1.11 Sentence constituents and basic sentence patterns

The previous sections presented the seven basic sentence patterns, noting major sentence constituents. Such constituents are as follows:

Subject	S
Verb	V
Subject Complement	SC
Direct Object	DO
Indirect Object	IO
Object Complement	OC
Adverbial Complement	AC

These constituents are, in a certain word order, assembled into the seven basic sentence patterns as follows:

Sentence Patterns		Verb Types	Examples
I	S+V	Intransitive	They are dancing. The fog disappeared.
II	S+V+SC	Linking	Joan is a doctor. The landscape is magnificent.
III	S+V+DO	Transitive	Gogh's paintings make a strong impression. Brightman has a heavenly voice.
IV	S+V+IO+DO	Ditransitive	He gave Jane a book. Lisa sent him an email.

V	S+V+DO+OC	Transitive	Sam made his parents happy. I found the film quite absorbing.
VI	S+V+AC	Intransitive	The concert lasted for two hours. He is in the classroom.
VII	S+V+DO+AC	Transitive	He put his car in the garage. The curator showed us into the National Gallery.

These patterns describe the different ways in which words and phrases can be put together to form grammatically correct sentences. The choice of sentence patterns depends on the intended meaning and the structure of the sentence. Here are seven sentence patterns:

1. Subject+Intransitive Verb (S V): This sentence pattern consists of a subject (NP: a noun or pronoun) followed by a verb (/VP/Predicate) (e.g., *She sings*).

2. Subject+Linking Verb+Complement (S V C): In this pattern, a subject is followed by a linking verb and a complement that describes the attribute, identification, or status of the subject (e.g., *Your research project is great*).

3. Subject+Transitive Verb+Direct Object (S V DO): This pattern is composed of a subject, a verb, and a direct object (a noun or pronoun), in that order (e.g., *I like apples*).

4. Subject+Verb+Indirect Object+Direct Object (S V IO DO): This pattern is made up of a subject, a verb, an indirect object (to whom or for whom something is done), and a direct object (the thing being acted upon), in that order (e.g., *Joan gave me a book*).

5. Subject+Verb+Direct Object+Object Complement (S V DO OC): In this pattern, a subject is followed by a verb, a direct object, and

an object complement which describes, identifies or characterizes the direct object, in that order (e.g., *They elected him mayor*, *She made her parents happy*).

6. Subject + Intransitive Verb + Adverbial Complement (S V AC): In this pattern, a subject is followed by a verb and an adverbial complement that provides necessary information about the situation described by a sentence, in that order (e.g., *She lives in Seoul*, *I live far from here*, *The BTS concert lasted for two hours*, *He went to Boston*, *He is here*).

7. Subject + Verb + Direct Object + Adverbial Complement (S V DO AC): This pattern comprises a subject, a verb, a direct object, and an adverbial complement (e.g., *He put his car in the garage*, *She kept her eyes on the kid*, *Keep/Get your hands off me*, *The curator showed us into the National Gallery*, *The doorman showed the guests into the drawing room* (Quirk, *et al.* 1985:56) (**the guests are into the drawing room*).

Sentence patterns are determined by the choice of the main verbs. Even a single verb may take different structures as in the following:

He sounded nervous. [S V SC]
He sounded the alarm. [S V DO]

He danced. [S V]
He danced the tango/a waltz. [S V DO]

They appointed a new director. [S V DO]
They appointed Son captain of Tottenham Hotspur. [S V DO OC]

He will make a good lawyer. [S V SC]
He made a delicious dish. [S V DO]

He made his wife a delicious dish. [S V IO DO]
He made his parents happy. [S V DO OC]

She will find a cure for cancer. [S V DO]
She found that a puppy was shivering under the stairs. [S V DO]
She found me my laptop. [S V IO DO]
She finds Galaxy watches very useful. [S V DO OC]

1.12 Semantic roles of the sentence constituents

Different constituents in a sentence carry unique meanings and fulfill specific semantic roles[15] that relate to the action or state conveyed by the verb.

1. Subject

A. **Agentive role**: The subject typically indicates the agent or doer of the action in sentences with an intransitive or transitive verb.

Son kicked a ball.
The old man walked slowly.

B. (External) **Causer role**: The inanimate subject causes an

15 The semantic roles, also known as theta roles or thematic roles, describe the different semantic functions that various constituents of a sentence can have with respect to the action or state expressed by the verb. Unfortunately, there is not a universally accepted standard list of semantic roles among researchers (cf. Fillmore (1968), O'Grady (1998), Kearns (2000), among others). However, most agree on a core set of roles essential for discussing the semantic roles or functions of noun phrases.

action or change of state, but may not perform it directly.

Hurricane Helene has killed at least 231 people.
The storm damaged several houses.

C. **Experiencer role**: The subject experiences or perceives an event or state such as a mental, psychological, or emotional state, which is relevant to cognition, perception, or feeling.

They felt happy.
Joan thinks/knows/feels that she will pass the exam.

D. **Identified role**: The subject refers to a specific entity that is identified in the sentence with a linking verb.

Joan is my English teacher.
Tim Robbins is the lead actor in *The Shawshank Redemption.*

E. **Characterized role**: The subject is described or characterized by the predicate of the sentence with a linking verb.

The kid is so cute/adorable.
Joan's voice sounded nervous.

F. **Affected role (theme, patient)**[16]: The subject plays a role as the entity which is affected by the action or state expressed by the verb or undergoes a change; it can sometimes emphasize the impact of the action on the entity.

The kid fell.
The government fell.
The window broke.
My watch has broken.

---

16 The terms *affected*, *theme*, and *patient* often overlap in discussions about semantic roles, and their usage can vary among scholars.

The soup is bubbling in the pot.

G. Instrument role: The subject is used as an instrument.

A stone broke the window.
The supercomputer finally solved the hard problem.

H. Empty or prop subject *it*: The subject *it* does not refer to a specific entity; instead, it serves as the subject of sentences expressing time, weather, distance, or vague situations.

It is raining.
It is three miles to the nearest gas station.
It is getting worse.

2. Subject complement and object complement

Subject complements and object complements can typically take the role of an attribute in a sentence by providing additional information that identifies or characterizes the subject or object.

A. Identification

She is *my teacher*$_{SC}$.
IU is *a singer-songwriter*$_{SC}$.
They elected him *president*$_{OC}$.
The CEO appointed Taylor *her secretary*$_{OC}$.

B. Characterization

He is *meticulous*$_{SC}$.
The story is *fascinating*$_{SC}$.
They consider him *intelligent*$_{OC}$.
I find the book *interesting*$_{OC}$.

3. Direct object

Semantic roles describe the relationship between noun phrases (including direct objects) and the action or state expressed by the verb.

A. Affected role (theme, patient): The direct object typically fulfills the role of the entity affected by the action expressed by the verb or undergoing a change of state.

She ate *the apple.*
He painted *the wall.*

B. Resultant role: A resultant role typically refers to the semantic role that denotes the outcome or result of an action or process expressed by the verb.

The company built *that beautiful house.*
Han Kang wrote *Sonyeoni onda* (*Human Acts*) in 2014.

C. Eventive role: The direct object can denote events. Nouns used as the direct object are typically derived from its verb form.

We enjoyed *a fifty-mile drive.*
They had *a long fight against injustice.*
The board rejected *their recommendations.*
They will make *a conclusion* soon.

D. Experiencer: The direct object can experience a mental, psychological, or emotional state.

The film shocked the students.
The story surprised Joan.

These roles help to analyze and understand how verbs interact with their direct objects to convey specific meanings in sentences.

4. Indirect object

A. **Recipient**: The recipient role pertains to verbs that denote a transfer of ownership or possession. It refers to the entity that receives something.

She gave *her son* a birthday gift.
The chef made *the guests* delicious dishes.

5. Verb

Verbs can be broadly categorized into two main types: dynamic verbs (also known as action verbs) and stative verbs.

A. **Dynamic verbs**: Dynamic verbs describe actions, activities, or changes over time, often involving movement (e.g., *walk*, *run*, *jump*, *swim*, *paint*, *build*, *write*, *grow*, *develop*, *change*).

B. **Stative verbs**: Stative verbs describe a state or condition rather than an action. They express a state of being, emotions, thoughts (mentally conceived), senses, or possession, as in the following examples:

- Mental and emotional states: believe, hate, know, like, realize, recognize, remember, suppose, think (to have a particular opinion or belief), understand, want.
- State of Being: be, seem, appear, look
- Emotions: love, (dis)like, hate, prefer, want, wish

- Senses: hear, see, smell, taste, feel
- Possession: have, possess, own, belong, lack
- Others: consist, fit, lack, matter, depend, contain, include

A dynamic verb can normally be used in the progressive form, while a stative verb cannot, as shown in the following:

Dynamic verbs

He *walked* along the lake. vs. He *was walking* along the lake.
Tom *wrote* a letter. vs. Tom *was writing* a letter.
They *swam* in the pool. vs. They *were swimming* in the pool.
They *listened* to his lecture. vs. They *were listening* to his lecture.

Stative verbs

He *is* a basketball player.
(*He is being a basketball player.)
The boss *is* impolite.
(The boss is being impolite.[17] 'behaving impolitely')
They *like* sports.
(*They are liking sports.)
The reporter *knows* the fact.
(*The reporter is knowing the fact. cf. He is getting to know it).
The couple *has* two houses in Boston.
(*The couple are having two houses in Boston. cf. They are having a good time in Boston)
Lisa *lacks* confidence.
*Lisa is lacking confidence.
I *see* a bird over there.
(*I'm seeing a bird over there.[18] cf. I'm looking at a bird over there)

---

17 The sentence indicates that at the current moment, his behavior or actions are characterized by impoliteness. This construction is commonly used to describe someone's temporary behavior or state.

18 The sentence is not grammatically correct when it states that the speaker

6. Adverbials

Adverbials play an important role in sentences by providing additional information about the place, direction, time, reason, manner, purpose, or frequency of actions or events described by verbs, as shown below:

1. Place: Adverbials that indicate where an action occurs
   They played the final match *at Seoul Olympic Stadium.*
   The couple built a high-quality house *in the village.*

2. Direction: Adverbials that indicate where an action is directed
   They walked *toward the park.*
   He went *to the airport.*

3. Time: Adverbials which denote when an action takes place
   They arrived *yesterday.*
   The team is leaving *tomorrow* for the final match.

4. Duration: Adverbials which indicate how long an action lasts
   He has worked *for two hours.*
   It is good to sleep *for seven to eight hours* per night.

5. Frequency: Adverbials that specify how often an action occurs
   They meet and study *occasionally* in the library.
   The earthquake occurs in this area *very frequently.*

6. Manner: Adverbials that denote how an action is performed
   Sarah Brightman sings *in a beautiful voice.*
   She responded *quite positively* to the interviewer.

---

has noticed it visually or is aware of the presence of a bird. In that case, it has to be *I see a bird over there*. (cf. *I'm seeing a doctor* means that the speaker currently has an appointment with a doctor or is in the process of consulting with one.)

7. Reason: Adverbials describing the causes of an event or situation.
   The final match was canceled *due to bad weather.*
   He became ill *because of eating contaminated food.*

8. Instrument: Adverbials specifying the means of an action.
   She sliced the bread *with a knife.*

9. Source: Adverbials specifying the origin of something; the starting point of a movement
   He fell *from the chair.*
   The film has been adapted *from a novel of the same title.*

10. Degree: Adverbials which indicate the intensity or extent of an action or state.
    The player jumped *very high.*
    She *entirely* agrees with your opinion.

11. Condition: Adverbials which express the circumstances under which an action will occur.
    If it rains, we will stay home.
    The water does not boil *under the conditions.*

12. Concession: Adverbials which introduce a contrast or unexpected situation relative to the main clause.
    Despite the rain, they went for a walk.

13. Assessment of the sentence: Adverbials which indicate an evaluation of the situation and express the speaker's attitude
    Fortunately, they found a solution to the problem.
    Surprisingly, she finished the project ahead of schedule.

14. logical connection: Adverbials which indicate linking units logically
    Amy is just 16; *therefore*, she is not eligible to vote.
    He completed the project successfully; *accordingly*, he got a bonus.

Adverbials can appear in various positions of a sentence and their diverse semantic roles contribute significantly to the complexity and nuance of language.

Exercises

1. Identify the subject and the verb constituent in each sentence.

   (1) We have read a book and discussed its theme.
   (2) Sylvia and her mother are traveling in Europe now.
   (3) They will arrive late due to traffic jams.
   (4) Sheila and her friends, excited about the upcoming concert, bought tickets weeks in advance.
   (5) Unlike the younger respondents, most of the older ones chose their diets primarily due to their concerns about health.
   (6) In the midst of the bustling town stands a quaint, cozy café that serves the best coffee.

2. Identify the operator in each sentence.

   (1) They will finish their project by Friday.
   (2) He has been waiting for the bus for over an hour.
   (3) They are going to stay in Europe for one month.
   (4) The manager is discussing the new project with the team.
   (5) He has been working tirelessly on his research paper.
   (6) They played basketball yesterday.

3. Convert the sentences in 2 to *yes-no* questions.

4. Convert the sentences in 2 to negative questions.

5. Identify adverbials and their semantic roles.

(1) Despite the heavy rain, they continued hiking.
(2) In the bustling city center, cars honked loudly.
(3) People hurriedly walked to their destinations.
(4) During the summer vacation, we traveled in Hawaii.
(5) With great enthusiasm, they worked on the upcoming school event.
(6) The outdoor concert was canceled because of the heavy rain.

6. Identify each sentence element (constituent).

(1) The castle stands on the hill.
(2) The meeting went smoothly.
(3) She was at home.
(4) The child behaved badly during the party.
(5) The outdoor concert lasted for two hours.
(6) She considers him a mentor.
(7) I found the book quite fascinating.
(8) They painted the room bright yellow.
(9) The chef cooked the steak medium rare.

Chapter 2

Word Classes

Objectives

- To understand various word classes
- To identify their characteristics and functions
- To explore their usage

Key words

open/closed classes; nouns; verbs (main verbs, auxiliary verbs); pronouns (personal, reflexive, reciprocal, demonstrative, interrogative, indefinite, relative); determiners; adjectives; adverbs; prepositions; conjunctions; case

As mentioned earlier, a sentence consists of words, which are its fundamental elements or building blocks. According to traditional English grammar books, words can be classified into various groups or classes, such as nouns, verbs (main verbs and auxiliary verbs), adjectives, adverbs, determiners, prepositions, and conjunctions. This classification is based on three major criteria: notional (semantic), formal (morphological), and distributional (syntactic) characteristics.

Meaning pertains to the semantic content of a word, encompassing the ideas or concepts it represents. Words are grouped into semantic classes such as nouns (e.g., *dog*), verbs (e.g., *run*), and adjectives (e.g., *happy*) based on their meanings. **Form** refers to the physical representation of a word, including its spelling, pronunciation, and

inflectional endings.[19] For example, the verb *teach* has different forms: *teach* (base form), *teaches* (present tense), and *taught* (past tense). Different word classes often have distinct forms, and **derivational suffixes,**[20] such as *-tion* (e.g., *action*) and *-ment* (e.g., *development*), are commonly used to form nouns. **Distribution** pertains to the syntactic environments in which words appear, including their roles in sentences. For example, verbs typically follow subjects in sentences (e.g., *I teach physics*). Understanding distributional patterns helps classify words based on their syntactic functions.

2.1 Word classes

1. notion (meaning)

Nouns refer to names of people, things, places, or occasions /events (e.g., *Joan*, *student*, *desk*, *classroom*, *picnic*, etc.).

Verbs denote actions, activities, or states (e.g., *run*, *jump*, *talk*; *have*, *want*, *consist*, *belong*, *lack*, etc.).

Adjectives express qualities, characteristics, or attributes of

---

19 Inflectional endings are suffixes added to a base word to convey grammatical information without changing the core meaning of the word. Those include *-(e)s* (plural of nouns: *cats*), *'s* (possessive for nouns: *the boy's*), *-s* (third person singular present of verbs: *runs*), *-ed* (past tense; past participle for verbs: *talked*), *-ing* (present participle of verbs: *playing*), *-er* (comparative of adjectives/adverbs: *taller*/*faster*), *-est* (superlative of adjectives/adverbs: *tallest*/*fastest*).

20 Derivational suffixes are added to a base word (root) to create a new word with a different meaning or to change the word class.

people or things (e.g., *soft*, *mild*, *brave*, *great*, *wonderful*, *careful*, *thin*, *good*, *meticulous*, etc.).

2. form

Nouns can be inflected in the plural form with *-s* (e.g., *chairs*, *books*, *candidates*) and some suffixes indicate specific noun classes (e.g., *criticism*, *decision*, *renovation*).

Verbs can be inflected in various ways: with the third person singular ending *-s* in the present tense, the *-ed* form for past and past participles, or the *-ing* form. Some suffixes also indicate specific verb classes (e.g., *criticize*, *dedicate*, *renovate*, *purify*, etc.).

Adjectives can have specific suffixes, as shown in examples like *careful*, *comfortable*, *economic*, *and rainy*.

3. distribution

Nouns can be modified by determiners or adjectives in phrases or sentences (e.g., *good students*, *the firefighter*).

(Main) Verbs can occur after auxiliaries, as shown in examples like *He can swim* and *He has finished the project*.

Adjectives can occur before a noun (e.g., *wonderful islands*, *beautiful nights*).

These criteria together help us understand and classify words in a systematic way.

2.1.1 Open and closed classes

Word classes, also known as parts of speech, may generally be classified as follows:

Major word classes

Word class	Examples
Open classes	
Nouns	Sam, Korea, pencil, happiness, information, sound
Main verbs	run, sound, mollify, give, make, last, put, eradicate
Adjectives	friendly, wonderful, harmless, normal, healthy
Adverbs	quite, early, late, sincerely, probably, quickly
Closed classes	
Pronouns	I, her, they, everybody, which, what, that
Auxiliary verbs	will, would, can, could, should, must, do
Prepositions	in, at, on, above, from, instead of, due to
Determiners[21]	a, the, this, that, all, such, some, each, first, three
Conjunctions	and, but, or, although, because, when, after

As in the above table, word classes are classified into two major groups: **open classes** and **closed classes**. The former typically include content words or lexical items that convey meaning, form the core vocabulary, and readily accept new members, such as nouns, main verbs, adjectives, and adverbs. The latter include function words that largely perform grammatical functions and that do not easily accept new members, such as pronouns, auxiliaries, prepositions,[22] determiners, and

21 Determiners consist of various word classes, including articles, demonstratives, numerals, etc.

22 Even though prepositions primarily express various functions like location, direction, time, etc., some prepositions also have lexical meanings, playing dual roles, as shown in *by the lake*, *by Han Kang*, *by bus*, *by mistake*, *by chance*, *by seven o'clock*, *by day*, *by the week* (Denham and Lobeck 2013).

conjunctions. Additionally, there are smaller, more specialized classes (or minor classes) of words.

Minor word classes

Word class	Examples
Interjections	oh, oops, bravo, wow, hooray, alas, phew, ugh, huh
Negative particle	not
Infinitive marker	to

2.1.2 Word classes and uses

Many words can belong to different word classes, depending on the context as follows:

> Those *sounds*$_N$ are noisy. vs. That *sounds*$_V$ good.
> *What*$_{Pron}$ do you like? vs. *What*$_D$ kind of music do you like?

Certain words share relationships based on their sounds, meanings, or spellings: homonyms, homographs, and homophones. Certain words show semantic relationships: synonym and antonym.

Relation Type\Criterion	Sound	Spelling	Meaning	Examples
homonyms	same	same	different	bat, bank, bear, fan
homographs	different	same	different	tear, bow, wind, lead
homophones	same	different	different	some/sum, son/sun
Relation Type\Criterion	Meaning			Examples
Synonyms	same or similar			flagrant/blatant
Antonyms	opposite			central/peripheral

Homonyms are words that share the same form and pronunciation but have different meanings, such as *bat* (a sports implement or a flying mammal) and *bank* (the side of a river or a financial institution). **Homographs** are words that have the same spelling but differ in meaning and pronunciation, like *lead* (to guide) and *lead* (a metal). **Homophones** are words that share the same pronunciation but have different meanings and spellings, such as *two* (numeral) and *too* (also). Examples include *their* (possessive) and *there* (adverb of place), as well as *flour* (baking ingredient) and *flower* (blooming plant). A **synonym** is a word with the same meaning as or very similar meaning to another word, as in *flagrant* vs. *blatant*, while an **antonym** is a word with an opposite meaning to another word, as in *central* vs. *peripheral.*

2.2 Nouns

2.2.1 Noun suffixes

Formal characteristics: Below are several common nominal (noun-forming) suffixes, along with examples of words formed with each suffix:

Nominal suffixes	Examples
(verb)-ment	refreshment, seduction, development, movement, statement, abridgment, excitement, retirement, treatment (from verbs)
(adjective)-ity, -ty	reality, activity, electricity, serenity, divinity, responsibility, generosity, certainty (from adjectives)
(adjective)-ness	happiness, darkness, kindness, carefulness, goodness, preparedness, fitness, sadness, sweetness (from adjectives)
(verb)-(a)tion, -ion, -sion	temptation, reduction, starvation, communication, suggestion, creation, fusion, confession, tension, transmission, decision, compulsion (from verbs)

(adjective)-ance/-ence	importance, brilliance, resistance, performance, appearance (from adjectives)
(verb)-er/or	teacher, worker, actor, visitor, actor, editor (from verbs)
(noun)-hood	childhood, brotherhood, neighborhood (from nouns)
(noun)-ship	friendship, leadership, citizenship (from nouns)
(noun)-ist	artist, scientist, journalist (from nouns)
(adjective)-ism	socialism, realism, materialism, romanticism, idealism, nationalism (from adjectives)
(noun)-ian, -an	musician, historian, American, Republican, Episcopalian, pedestrian, Puritan (from nouns)
(verb)-age	storage, package, marriage (from verbs)

These suffixes are added to verbs, adjectives, and nouns to create new nouns, covering a wide variety of meanings and concepts.

2.2.2 Noun subclasses

Nouns can be subclassified as follows:

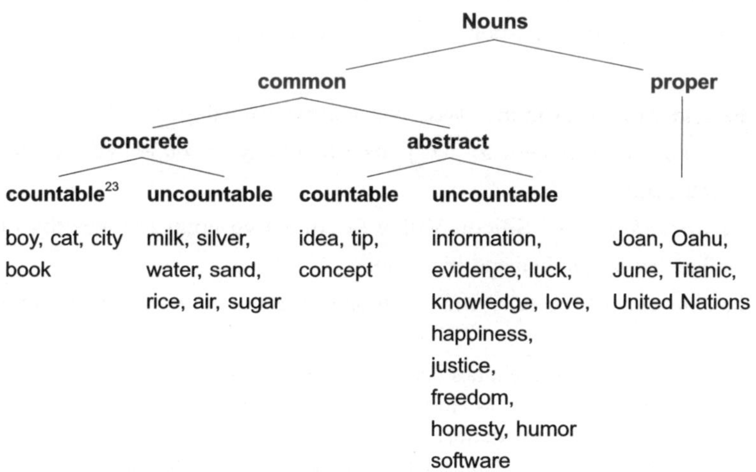

Here are explanations and examples of different classes of nouns. Nouns can be classified into common nouns and proper nouns.

1. Proper nouns

Proper nouns refer to specific names of people, places, events, organizations, or things. Their initial letters are capitalized, unlike common nouns. Proper nouns often refer to unique entities, such as:

Person: Joan, Rachel, Dr. Hawking
Place: Boston, Chicago, New York, Mount Everest
Events: Easter, Thanksgiving Day, Christmas
Organization: Microsoft, NASA, United Nations, Washington Post
Thing: iPhone, Coca-Cola, Titanic

Conversion to common nouns: Proper nouns can often function as common nouns. This usually occurs when we use the name of a family or a famous person in the plural sense:

There are *two Steves* in my class. (two students named Steve)
I have known *the Jacobs* for ten years. (the family or couple with the last name *Jacob*).
The *Rockefellers* of Silicon Valley (a collective noun for wealthy or influential people in a specific sector)
The *Einsteins* of the scientific community (prominent scientists as well-

23 Count nouns refer to entities that can be counted as individual items, while noncount nouns refer to entities seen as a whole or mass, not separate items. Count nouns denote individual countable entities and not an undifferentiated mass. Noncount nouns denote an undifferentiated mass or continuum (Quirk 1985:246).

known or influential as Albert Einstein)
The *Hemingways* of the literary world (great writers in the style of Ernest Hemingway)

2. Common nouns

Common nouns refer to general names for people, places, things, or ideas. They are not specific and are not capitalized unless they begin a sentence. Based on their properties, common nouns are subclassified as concrete or abstract nouns, and these are further divided into countable (entities that can be counted as individual items) or uncountable nouns (entities that cannot be counted individually).

Person: child, doctor, student, teacher
Place: city, country, park
Thing: table, book, car
Idea or quality: happiness, courage, freedom, honor, pride, justice (abstract)

A. Concrete nouns

Concrete nouns refer to objects or substances that have a physical existence or form and can be perceived by the senses (*sight, hearing, touch, taste, or smell*).

Objects: pen, table, chair, computer
(countable: used with *a*(*n*) and in plural forms)
Living beings: dog, cat, bug, tree, flower
(countable: used with *a*(*n*) and in plural forms)
Substances: rice, sugar, milk, water, air, wind, light, gold, silver[24]

24 Concepts or entities, as well as these substances, are called mass nouns.

(uncountable: not used with *a*(*n*) or in plural forms, but used with quantifiers like *a little*, *much*, *a lot of*, etc.)

B. Abstract nouns

Abstract nouns refer to ideas, concepts, qualities, emotions, or states that are not tangible and cannot be perceived through the senses.

Ideas/concepts: belief, thought, justice, love, freedom, democracy, time; wisdom, information, evidence, luck, software
Qualities: beauty, kindness, loyalty, conscience; patience, courage, generosity, creativity, intelligence, honesty, humor
Emotions: anger, fear, grief, sadness, happiness, pleasure

There is a general tendency for abstract nouns to be uncountable. For example, abstract nouns like *wisdom*, *luck*, *information*, *evidence*, *software*, *honesty*, and *humor* are all uncountable (mass) nouns, so they do not have plural forms and are not used with indefinite articles like *a* or *an*. These nouns can be used with partitive expressions (such as *a piece of*, *a bit of*, *a lot of*, *a sense of* etc.) to indicate a portion or a specific quantity of the noun. On the other hand, abstract nouns like *belief*, *thought*, *justice*, etc. can

---

They cannot usually be counted, pluralized as discrete units, or separated into individual elements. Mass nouns can be either concrete nouns, which are perceptible physically, or abstract nouns, which are intangible or imperceptible physically. Countable and uncountable nouns like *brick* have 'dual class membership' (Quirk, *et al.* 1985:246). Nouns such as *pig* fall into the category of concrete nouns (accessible to the senses, observable, measurable, etc.), while nouns like *difficulty* belong to the category of abstract nouns (typically nonobservable and nonmeasurable) (Quirk, *et al.* 1985:247).

have plural forms as in *Some members hold right-wing beliefs; others hold left-wing beliefs* and *Do you have any thoughts on how to spend the money?* Among the abstract nouns denoting qualities listed above, *beauty*, *kindness*, *loyalty*, and *conscience* can also be used as countable nouns in certain contexts, while the others usually cannot.

3. Conversion from uncountable to countable nouns

Uncountable nouns refer to substances, concepts/abstract qualities, or entities that cannot be counted as discrete units or separated into individual elements. Examples are *blood*, *water*, *milk*, *oil*, *clay*, *oxygen*, *steel*, *gold*, etc. (nouns denoting material); *bravery*, *valor*, *enthusiasm*, *humanity*, *knowledge*, *music*, *education*, *homework*, *weather*, etc. (concepts/abstract nouns); *jewelry*, *clothing*, *baggage*, *luggage*, *poetry*, *furniture*, *equipment*, *machinery*, etc. (collective nouns).

Some uncountable nouns can be converted into countable nouns in special contexts. Uncountable nouns may be treated as countable when referring to different types or varieties of something.

We tried *three different cheeses* at the wine tasting.
The restaurant offers *a selection of cheeses* on its appetizer platter
  (several varieties or types of cheese)
We tried *three different beers* at the pub last night.
  (different types or brands)

Uncountable nouns can also be treated as countable when they denote specific units in context.

I'll take *three coffees*, two black and one with milk.

We ordered *three coffees* for the office meeting. (three servings/cups)
We ordered two beers at the bar. (two servings/bottles/cups)

Many nouns can be tricky because they can function as both countable and uncountable, depending on the context. Some nouns change meaning, depending on whether they are countable or uncountable.

I need *paper* to write a letter. (material; uncountable)
I have *two papers* to write for my class. (individual pieces of writing; countable)
Jenifer has long *hair*. (substance; uncountable)
There are *two hairs* in my soup. (Individual strands of hair; countable)
I don't have *time* to go to the gym today. (general concept; uncountable)
How many *times* have you visited the museum? (specific occasions; countable)
The window is made of *glass*. (material; uncountable)
I broke *two glasses*. (drinking vessels; countable)

Some pairs of nouns, such as *journey* vs. *travel* or *fruit* vs. *vegetable*, are treated differently in terms of countability, as follows:

Life is *a journey* to the unknown. (countable)
They had *two separate journeys* across Europe. (specific trips)
Travel is one of my favorite activities. (general concept; uncountable)
We used to do a lot of *travel* for work before the pandemic. (the overall activity or concept of going from one place to another)
I eat a lot of *fruit*. (the general category of food; uncountable)
She likes *fruit* and *vegetables.*
I bought three *vegetables* at the market. (specific types; countable)

4. Collective nouns

Among the uncountable nouns listed above, *jewelry*, *clothing*, *baggage*, *luggage*, *poetry*, *furniture*, *equipment*, and *machinery* are collective nouns that refer to groups or collections of things, which are treated as singular despite consisting of many individual parts. They typically refer to items or things grouped together as a whole. Also, *audience*, *committee*, *family*, *team*, *and government* are all collective nouns. These refer to groups of people or entities that are treated as a single unit, even though they consist of multiple individuals or members. In British English, these nouns can generally take either singular or plural verbs and pronouns.

The committee is/are meeting tomorrow. (BE; *is* preferred in AE)
The government is/are implementing new policies
The team is/are preparing for the championship game.

The word *police* takes plural verbs. Collective nouns like *team* or *committee* take singular verb forms when used with the verb *consist of* as follows:

The police *are* investigating the case.
The police *have* arrested him for possessing a gun.
The team/committee *consists* of 11 members.

5. Quantifiers and nouns

Countable and uncountable nouns usually take different quantifiers, and quantifiers like *some*, *plenty of*, *a lot of*, *lots of*, etc. can occur before both countable and uncountable nouns.

Quantifiers are words or phrases that provide information about the quantity or amount of something, without specifying an exact number.

- **Countable nouns** can take *many*, (*a*) *few*, *several*; *a lot of/lots of*, *some*, *all*, *none of*, and so on as follows:

Many people attended the event.
There were *few cars* on the road.
I have *a few books* to read.
Jane bought *several gifts*.
Some students are absent.
All the chairs are occupied.
None of the cookies are left.

- **Uncountable nouns** can take *much*, (*a*) *little*; *a lot of/lots of*, *some*, *all*, *none of*, and so on as follows:

I don't have *much time*.
There is *little water* in the bottle.
I need *a little sugar* for my coffee.
I would like to have *some milk*.
All the information is here.
None of the butter is left.

2.2.3 Number: regular vs. irregular forms of nouns

Countable nouns can be counted individually and have distinct forms for singular and plural. The regular plural form is typically formed by adding *-(e)s* to the singular form. However, there are some irregular plural forms.

1. Regular formation

-s affixation: For most nouns (e.g., *students*, *books*, *cars*, *dogs*).
-es affixation: For nouns ending in *-s*, *-x*, *-z*, *-sh*, *-ch* (e.g., *buses*, *boxes*, *quizzes*, *wishes*, *churches*).

2. Irregular formation

Irregular plural forms frequently reflect historical remnants, older English forms, or loanwords that have carried over into modern English.

- **Vowel change**: *man - men, woman - women, foot - feet, tooth - teeth, goose - geese; mouse - mice, louse - lice*
- **Specific plural suffixes**: *child - children, ox - oxen, brother - brethren*
- **Same forms (isomorphs)**: Some nouns have the same form in singular and plural (*deer*, *sheep*).
- **Loanwords**: *analysis - analyses, crisis - crises, criterion - criteria, curriculum - curricula, datum - data, phenomenon - phenomena, stimulus - stimuli; fungus - fungi/funguses, index - indices/indexes, cactus - cacti/cactuses/cactus; barracks, salmon, series, species* (isomorphs)
- **Compound nouns**: *father-in-law - fathers-in-law, notary public - notaries public, passer-by - passers-by; man servant - men servants, woman doctor - women doctors; forget-me-not - forget-me-nots, girlfriend - girlfriends, grown-up - grown-ups, stand-by - stand-bys*

2.2.4 Gender

Although most nouns in English, unlike French or German, do not have distinctions in gender such as masculine, feminine, and non-personal, there are some nouns that show gender distinction. English assigns gender based on natural gender.

- **Masculine - feminine**: *father - mother, son - daughter, king - queen, man - woman, bridegroom - bride*; *bull - cow, rooster - hen*; *actor - actress, prince - princess, hero - heroine*
- **Non-personal**: Objects and abstract concepts usually have no gender. (*book, chair, idea, opinion*)
- **Gender-neutral terms**: In present-day English, there is a tendency to use gender-neutral words to avoid gender distinction: *partner/spouse* instead of *husband/wife*, *flight attendant* instead of *steward/stewardess*, *firefighter* instead of *fireman/ firewoman*

2.2.5 Case

Case marks the grammatical function or role of a noun phrase and also indicates grammatical relations between noun phrases in a sentence. Nouns have two primary cases: the common case and the genitive case (also known as the possessive case). The former, as its name indicates, refers to the form of a noun that is not marked for a specific grammatical case.

1. **Common case**: This is used for the subject, complement (subject /object), and object (direct/indirect) of a sentence as the unmarked form, regardless of singular or plural, as follows:

   My *cat(s)* jumped over the fence.
   It is (They are) *my cat(s)*.
   He usually tends *my cat(s)*.

He gave my *cat(s)* some food.

2. **Genitive case (possessive case)**: This usually indicates ownership or possession, showing that one noun belongs to or is dependent on another noun. Genitive case forms take an apostrophe + *s* for singular nouns, while genitive forms of plural nouns ending in *s* take only an apostrophe, as follows:

The teacher's article (The teachers' articles) dealt with climate justice.
The child's (The children's) scooter(s) is (are) very convenient.

The genitive forms above have a determinative function, as they specify or determine the noun they precede, indicating possession or association.

On the other hand, the genitive forms can be used independently or function as non-determinatives. Independent (or free) genitives consist of nouns (or pronouns) in the genitive case that stand alone without the noun they possess, relying instead on context for clarity, as follows:

- **independent function**

I visited *Sarah's*. (*Sarah's* implies ownership of a place without explicitly stating what it is; It could refer to her house, shop, etc.)
The boys played at the park, then they went to *Tim's*.
I can't find my keys, but I found *Becky's*.
John's is the best pizza in town.
I don't want to borrow Lisa's book; I'll take *Karen's* instead.
I like that dress better than *Suzan's*.
I usually have my hair cut at *Helen's*.
Is that dog *Sarah's*?
A: What's your name?
B: *Mine* is Rebecca. (pronoun)

The effectiveness of independent genitives lies in the relevant context. For example, during a conversation about pets, saying *Is that dog Sarah's?* conveys the notion of ownership. The word *Sarah's* functions independently, referring to the person already mentioned in the context of the conversation, thereby eliminating redundancy.

That is clearly an idea of *John's* (= … one of John's ideas.)
He is a friend of *Joan's/mine*. (= … one of Joan's/my friends.)
The party is at *Michael's* tonight. (= … at Michael's house.)

2.3 Main verbs

2.3.1 Verb suffixes

Formal characteristics: Below are several common verb-forming suffixes, along with examples of words formed with each suffix:

Nominal suffixes	Examples
(A/N) + -ize/-ise	familiarize, modernize, organize, realize (from adjectives and nouns)
(N) + -ify, -fy	beautify, intensify, satisfy, signify (from nouns)
(A/N) + -ate	activate, circulate, differentiate, originate (from adjectives, nouns)
(A/N) + -en	brighten, soften, darken, hasten (from adjectives, nouns)

2.3.2 Forms of the verb

Main verbs are used in various forms as follows:

Forms		Regular	Irregular
base form		**walk**	**drive**
present form	**3rd person sg.**	walk-***s***	drive-***s***
	the others	walk	drive
past form		walk-***ed***	dr**o**ve
participle form	**-ing**	walk-***ing***	driv-***ing***
	-ed/-en	walk-***ed***	driv-***en***

1. The base form is the one typically listed in dictionary entries.
2. The third-person singular present form (also known as the *-s* form) is created by adding the suffix *-s* to the base form.
3. The other present forms are identical to the base form.[25]
4. The past or past participle form (also known as the *-ed* form) is constructed by adding the *-ed* suffix to the base form for regular verbs; it is formed in various complex ways for irregular verbs.
5. The present participle (*-ing* form) is formed by adding the suffix *-ing* to the base form.

2.3.3 Irregular verbs

Irregular verbs are verbs that do not follow the regular pattern of conjugation. Unlike regular verbs, which typically form their past tense and past participle by adding *-ed* or *-d* to the base form (e.g., *walk/walked/walked*), irregular verbs have unique forms for their past tense and past participle. These forms often do not follow

25 Actually we have four different forms of regular verbs.

a predictable pattern and must be learned individually. Common examples of irregular verbs include *eat* (*ate/eaten*) and *see* (*saw/seen*). Irregular verbs can be divided into seven groups, based on the characteristics of past forms and *-ed*/past participle forms of irregular verbs, as shown in the following table:

Classes of irregular verbs[26]

Class	Examples	Characteristics
I	put put put, hit hit hit	no change
II	build built built, make made made	consonant change
III	hold held held, win won won	vowel change
IV	begin began begun, run ran run	complex vowel change
V	keep kept kept, tell told told	vowel change, *–t*/*-d* addition
VI	see saw seen, drive drove driven	vowel change, *-en* addition
VII	show showed shown/showed, swell swelled swollen/swelled	two suffixes (& vowel change)

They show various characteristics, such as no change, consonant change, vowel change, *-t*/*-d*/*-en* addition, etc.

Except for regular and irregular verbs, there are anomalous verbs (*be* and *go*), which refer to verbs that have exceptional forms or conjugation patterns that do not fit regular or typical irregular verb patterns. The verb *go* has the conjugation *go-went-gone*,[27] while the verb *be* has various forms, as shown in the table below.

26 Base forms, past forms, and past participle forms of irregular verbs are listed in Appendix.

27 The past form of *go* (*went*) was formed though **suppletion**, which refers to the phenomenon in which a word has different forms that originate from different roots or stems rather than being derived from a single, consistent base form. The past form comes from the Old English verb *wendan* (meaning 'to go').

Anomalous verb *be (main verb vs. linking verb)*

Person	Singular	Plural	Tense
1st	am was	are were	present past
2nd	are were	are were	present past
3rd	is was	are were	present past

2.4 Pronouns

Pronouns replace nouns or noun phrases to avoid repetition or refer to previously mentioned people or things. They promote linguistic simplicity by reducing redundancy and making sentences more efficient and concise.

A: *John and Joan* went to Boston.
B: When did *they* go there?

Pronouns are important in clear and cohesive writing and communication. There are several types of pronouns, such as personal pronouns, possessive pronouns, reflexive pronouns, reciprocal pronouns, demonstrative pronouns, indefinite pronouns, interrogative pronouns, and relative pronouns.

2.4.1 Personal pronouns

Personal pronouns refer to specific persons or things, which generally have distinctions in person, number, case, and/or gender.

Number/Case Person/Gender		Singular		Plural	
		Subjective	Objective	Subjective	Objective
1st person		I	me	we	us
2nd person		you	you	you	you
3rd person	masculine	he	him	they	them
	feminine	she	her		
	non-personal	it	it		

The subjective and objective case forms are used in the subject and object positions of a finite clause,[28] respectively, as shown in the following:

Joan thinks that *she*$_{S}$ can finish the project successfully.
The teacher congratulated *them*$_{DO}$ on their results.
Why don't you talk about *him*$_{pC}$?

The subjective case form is also used in the subject complement position in formal style. In less formal style, the objective case form is commonly used as the subject complement.

This is *he/she*. It was *she* who called Bill.
A: Who's there? B: It's *me*.
It was *her* who called Bill.

The third person masculine and feminine forms of personal pronouns are used for human beings or animals, such as *dogs* and *cats*, based on natural gender distinctions. Non-personal things or objects, such as *boats*, *ships*, or *cars*, may take the

28 A finite clause includes a verb that marks tense, number, and person. These features are relevant to personal pronouns, but not to nouns. For nouns, only tense and number are relevant.

feminine form (*she*) of personal pronouns. Otherwise, *it* or *they* is used, depending on whether the noun is singular or plural.

She (= Your car) is so fast. Fill *her* up.
The Mayflower set sail from England in 1620, and *she* bravely crossed the Atlantic, carrying the Pilgrims to a new world.

Traditionally, third-person masculine pronouns have been used when a person's gender is unknown or when referring to both genders collectively, especially in formal contexts. Some people prefer gender-neutral alternatives like *he or she*, *(s)he*, or *they*.

If a student forgets *his or her* homework, *he or she* should speak with the teacher about making up the assignment.
Every employee must submit *his or her* report by Thursday.
The winner of the contest will be announced tomorrow, and *(s)he* will receive a certificate of achievement.
If anyone has any questions, *they* should feel free to ask. (less formal)

The following table presents possessives.

Possessives (possessive pronouns[29])

Case		(Genitive)			
Subclass		Possessive Determiner		Possessive Pronouns	
Function		Determinative[33]		Independent	
Person/Gender	Number	Singular	Plural	Singular	Plural
1st person		my	our	mine	ours
2nd person		your		yours	

29 Possessive pronouns have two sets of forms:one set has a determinative function and the other has an independent function (Quirk, *et al.* 1985:346).

3rd person	masculine	his	their	his	theirs
	feminine	her		hers	
	non-personal	its		--	

Genitive forms of personal pronouns are divided into two groups—possessive determiners and possessive pronouns—based on their functions (determinative and independent). Possessive determiners have a determinative function and precede the nouns they determine, while possessive pronouns have an independent function and stand alone without a following noun, as follows:

This notebook is *mine*. That notebook is *yours*. (independent function)
This is *my* notebook. That is *your* notebook. (Determinative function)

2.4.2 Reflexive pronouns[30]

The reflexive pronouns end in *self* for the singular and *selves* for the plural, as shown in the following:

Person/Gender \ Number		Singular	Plural
1st person		myself	ourselves
2nd person		yourself	yourselves
3rd person	masculine	himself	themselves
	feminine	herself	
	non-personal	itself	

When the subject and the object of a sentence refer to the same person or thing within the same clause, the object takes a reflexive pronoun, as follows:

30 Another term of determinative is **dependent** (Nelson and Greenbaum 2016).

He$_i$ dedicated *himself*$_i$ (**herself*$_j$) to scientific research all his life.
She$_i$ blamed *herself*$_i$ for the mistake.

The fixed expressions *by myself/yourself/themselves* etc. mean 'alone; without help from anybody.'

They$_i$ managed to finish the project by *themselves*$_i$.
I enjoy spending time *by myself* when I need to recharge.

In the following examples, personal pronouns are used instead of reflexive pronouns.

They$_i$ put their$_i$ bags *in front of/behind/beside them*$_i$ (*themselves).
The sounds you hear *around you* (*yourself) in the forest can help ease your mind.
As you walk through the city, the sounds you hear *around you* (*yourself)—from honking horns to people talking—create a bustling, lively atmosphere.
You need to take an umbrella *with you* (*yourself), just in case it rains.

The reflexive pronouns have two main functions. They are used either to emphasize the subject or object of the sentence (emphatic function) or to refer back to a noun or pronoun previously mentioned in the same clause (reflexive function).

1. Reflexive function

She devoted *herself* to environmental protection.
Steve prepared *himself* for bad news.
Joan introduced *herself* proudly.

2. Emphatic function

I did it *myself.*
She made the decision *herself.*
He *himself* knew what he would do.
The applicant did not understand the question *itself.*

2.4.3 Reciprocal pronouns

Reciprocal pronouns are used to express a mutual action or relationship between two or more people or things, indicating that the subjects are performing an action mutually. The primary reciprocal pronouns are *each other* and *one another*, with the former being more common than the latter in less formal contexts. These pronouns are not typically used as the subject of a sentence. Their genitive forms are *each other's* and *one another's*.

They hugged *each other/one another.*
Jade and I have known *one another* for years.
Joan and I send text messages to *each other/one another* every day.
They were gazing into *each other's/one another's* faces in amazement.
They supported *each other's/one another's* dreams through thick and thin.

Words like *meet* or *marry* are not normally used with *each other/ one another.*

Jason and Emily met and married (**each other*) in 2005.

2.4.4 Demonstrative pronouns

Demonstrative pronouns are used to point to specific things or people, often in relation to the speaker's location, which include *this*, *that*, *these*, and *those*. *This* is used for a thing or person close to the speaker, while *that* refers to a thing or person farther away from the speaker.

singular	plural	referent
this	these	a thing or person close to the speaker
that	those	a thing or person farther away from the speaker

This is very interesting.
These are very impressive.
That is so fast.
Those are very expensive.

They are used as determiners when preceding a noun as follows: .

This book is very interesting.
These paintings are very impressive.
That car is so fast.
Those cars are very expensive.

2.4.5 Interrogative pronouns

Interrogative pronouns are used to ask questions about people, things, or situations. They help in identifying or obtaining specific information. The primary interrogative pronouns are listed in the table below:

Use \ Case	Subjective	Genitive	Objective
Personal	who	whose	whom
(Non-)personal	which	—	which
Non-personal	what	—	what

Who is coming to the party?
Whom did you invite to the wedding?
(*whom* is more formal and less common in everyday speech)
Whose keys are these? (determinative genitive)
Whose are these keys? (independent genitive)

Which do you prefer, coffee or tea?
Which of Gogh's paintings is the most impressive?
(independent genitive)
Which paintings are more impressive, Gogh's or Monet's?
(determinative genitive)

What brought you here?
What is your favorite film?
What do you study?
What are you doing on weekends? (independent genitives)
What exercise do you do on weekends? (determinative genitive)
What book are you reading these days? (determinative genitive)

As shown in the examples above, *whose*, *which*, and *what* can also be used as determiners.

2.4.6 Indefinite pronouns

Indefinite pronouns refer to non-specific people, things, or ideas. They are used when the identity or quantity is usually unknown or irrelevant. Unlike pronouns such as *he*, *she*, or *it*, indefinite pronouns are more vague, non-specific, and gender-neutral. Below are some examples.

All (the students)were surprised at the announcement.
All I want is peace.

Many (students) have signed up for the course.
Several (students) have already completed the project.
Only *a few* (students) completed the assignment on time.
Few (students) understand the complexity of the issue.
One of the options is better suited for the task.
I bought two shirts; *one* is blue, and *the other* is red.
None of the proposed solutions were feasible.
There was *none* left.
None of his kids have got any sense.
Each of the members will receive a certificate.
Each (member) will receive a certificate.
More (members) will join us for dinner later this evening.
Both (students) are ready for the presentation.
Either (option) will be suitable for the task.
Everyone/everybody enjoyed the concert.
Everything is ready for the party.
Nothing is more important than family.

The italicized examples above are indefinite pronouns, and they function as indefinite determiners when followed by a noun in parentheses.

Here are some common types of indefinite pronouns: the *any*-type and *some*-type pronouns, which typically show distributional contrast.

• *Some*-type and *any*-type indefinite pronouns

Some-type indefinite pronouns are generally used in affirmative sentences and in situations expecting a positive answer in a question, while any-type indefinite pronouns are used in negative sentences and questions.

Some-type indefinite pronoun	Any-type indefinite pronoun
some	any
somebody	anybody
someone	anyone
something	anything
somewhere	anywhere
used in affirmative sentences & in situations expecting a positive/yes answer in a question	used usually in negative sentences, questions

Some-type indefinite pronouns

Some of the cake is still in the fridge.
Some of the customers are waiting in line for their orders..
Would you like *some?*
Somebody left a message for you.
Someone left the keys on the table.
I need *something* to drink.
We should find *somewhere* to eat.

Any-type indefinite pronouns

A: Do you have any milk? B: I don't have *any.*
I don't have any more questions. Do you have *any?*
Is *anyone* else coming to the party?
I don't know *anyone* who can play the guitar as well as you.
I don't have *anything* to add to the discussion.
We don't have *anywhere* to stay.
If you want, you can take *any* of these.
Anybody can learn to play the piano if they practice regularly.
Anywhere is fine for our meeting.

As seen in the last three examples, *any*-type indefinite pronouns can be used in affirmative sentences as well.

Let us consider the following sentences.

Did anyone notice the new painting? (This broadly inquires if there was any awareness of the new painting.)

Did someone notice the new painting? (This implies an expectation that at least one person probably noticed the new painting.)

In everyday use, both sentences can often be used interchangeably, but *anyone* has a broader implication, while *someone* suggests that at least one person probably did.

Indefinite pronouns can be singular, plural, or both, depending on the pronoun and the context. For example, *everyone*, *someone*, and *everything* are singular, while *several* and *both* are plural, as in the following examples:

Someone left *his or her (their*: informal) umbrella here.

Everything is ready for the party.

Several have already finished their assignments.

Few have been as dedicated as she is.

Many indefinite pronouns may be followed by post-modifier.

Anyone with a key can enter the room.

Everybody in the office was invited to the party.

Nothing important was mentioned during the meeting.

Somebody from the marketing department should handle this.

Something special about this painting caught my eye — it's so unique.

She wanted to do *something* special for her birthday this year.

Someone else must have left the lights on because I turned them off earlier.

If you don't want the job, I'll find *someone else* to take care of it.

None of us knew about the surprise party until the last minute.

I've spoken with *some* in the office about the project.
Either of them would be a great choice for the project.
You can choose *either* of them to fill the position.
Many of the words on the list were misspelled, so we had to correct them.

2.4.7 Relative pronouns

Relative pronouns introduce relative clauses and connect them to the main clause. They function as both conjunctions and pronouns. The relative pronouns *who* and *which* have distinctions in case, as shown below:

Use \ Case	Subjective case	Objective case	Genitive case
personal	who	whom	whose
non-personal	which	which	whose
(non)personal	that	that	—
nonpersonal	what	what	—

1. Relative clause formation

a. He has a lot of interesting books. The books are easy to read.
→ He has a lot of interesting books which/that are easy to read.
b. I know the student. The student is majoring in linguistics.
→ I know the student who/that is majoring in linguistics.
c. I met a woman. The woman's brother works in the same company.
→ I met a woman whose brother works in the same company.
d. I know the student. The student's major is robotics.
→ I know the student whose major is robotics.
e. I remember those whom (formal)/who (informal)/that we met in Paris.

In each case, the relative pronoun refers back to the antecedent (the noun or pronoun the relative clause modifies). The choice of relative pronouns depends on its role in the clause and the nature of the antecedent.

2. Nominal relative clauses

The relative pronoun *what* introduces a nominal relative clause, which does not have an antecedent. *What* means 'the thing which' and *what*-clauses can function as a subject, subject complement, direct object, or propositional complement. Some examples are:

What I'm going to do is (to) go over the plan and make sure everything is ready. (subject)
That's *what I thought*. (subject complement)
I don't understand *what you mean*. (direct object)
He told her *what he thought*. (direct object)
Listen to *what he is saying*. (propositional complement)

3. Types of relative clauses

There are two types of relative clauses.

- Restrictive relative clauses: These identify the noun (antecedent) they modify.

  Those *who usually have a good sleep* live longer.
  The book *that I borrowed* is on the table.

- Non-restrictive relative clauses: These provide additional information about the noun. In non-restrictive relative clauses, a comma is used before a relative pronoun (except for *that*).

  This is Professor Donegan, *who is teaching phonology*.
  The artist, *whose paintings were displayed in the gallery*, is famous.

The Eiffel Tower, *which is in Paris*, is a famous landmark.
The house, *whose roof is painted orange*, is very expensive.

4. Preference for *that* in restrictive relative clauses

When relative pronouns follow quantifiers like *all*, *each*, *none*, *everybody/thing*, *somebody/thing*, *anybody/thing*, *little*, *nothing*, *only*, etc., and superlatives, *that* is more natural and preferred over *who*, *whom*, or *which*. This usage typically occurs in restrictive relative clauses. Below are some examples:

All *that* glitters is not gold.
He explained everything *that* was unclear.
There's something *that* I need to tell you.
There's nothing *that* I can do about it.
Nothing *that* you say will change my mind.
Every book *that* I borrowed is due tomorrow.
Each of the students *that* passed the exam was given a certificate.
Anybody *that* works hard deserves a reward.
None of those people *that* I know has seen this movie.
He is the only person *that* I trust completely.
This is the only book *that* I consider the best I've ever read.
This is the most interesting book *that* I've read this year.

2.4.8 (Indefinite) Pronoun *one*

The (indefinite) pronoun *one* can have three distinct uses: numerical *one*, generic *one*, and substitute *one*.

1. Numerical *one*

Determinative function: The numerical *one* determines the following noun.

At the end of the class, *one* student asked the teacher two questions.

The head of a noun phrase: The **numerical one** functions as the head of a noun phrase.

One of the students volunteered to help clean up after the event.
One is not enough.
Only *one* can win the prize.
If you choose *one*, I'll choose the other.
There is only *one* who can do that.

2. Generic *one*

The **generic one** refers to people in general, rather than a specific individual. It is used to make general statements or suggestions about typical behaviors or rules, give advice, or express universal truths, rules, or observations without specifying a particular person. In informal style, personal pronouns like *we*, *you*, or *they* are more commonly used than the generic *one*.

One should be polite to others.
If *one* wants to succeed, *one* must work hard.
One often learns more from failure than from success.
One must consider consequences before taking action.
One must consider various factors before making a decision.
One should listen to the voice for climate justice, or else future generations may be endangered.

3. Substitute *one*

The **substitute *one*** is used to replace a noun which has already been mentioned or implied. It functions similarly to other pronouns in that it refers back to something previously established in the context.

I don't like the red shirt, but I do like the blue *one*.
She wanted the red dress, but she ended up buying the green *one*.
He asked for a regular coffee, but the barista gave him a decaf *one*.
I didn't like the first movie, so I watched the second *one*.
I like the red shoes better than the blue *ones*.
I'll take the new *ones*; the old *ones* are too small.
I don't like these shirts; I prefer the striped *ones*.
The large chairs are more comfortable than the small *ones*.

2.4.9 Numerals

Numerals are symbols or words used to represent numbers. They can be categorized into a few types based on their function and form.

1. Cardinal numerals

Cardinal numerals represent quantity. They answer the question *How many?* and are used to count objects or denote an amount (*one, two, three, twenty, seventy-five, one hundred*).

I have *three* apples. (determiner)
The library has over *two thousand* books. (determiner)
Three is enough. (pronoun)

2. Ordinal numerals

Ordinal numerals indicate order in a sequence of entities. They answer questions like *Which one in the series of books do you recommend?* and are used to describe the rank or position of items (*first, second, third, twenty-first, seventy-fifth, one hundredth*).

She finished in *third* place. (determiner)
The *first* is concerned with social issues.
You should read the *first* two chapters before the class begins.

3. Fraction(al numerals)

Fractional numerals represent parts of a whole and are used to denote divisions or ratios (1/2 *(one-half)*, *3/4 (three-fourths)*, *7/9 (seven-ninths)*)

Numerals as pronouns: avoiding repetition

Numerals can function as pronouns, replacing specific quantities or numbers in a sentence. This helps avoid repetition and keeps sentences concise by substituting nouns or noun phrases which have already been mentioned or are understood from the context.

I have two pens; do you need *one*?
She bought two dresses, but she decided to return *one.*
There are several books on the table. You can take *one* if you want.
We have five chairs, but just *two* are comfortable.
I preferred two of the proposals.
The resolution demanding the lifting of martial law was passed unanimously, with 190 votes in favor out of *190* present.

2.5 Determiners

2.5.1 (Sub)classes of determines

Determiners are words that introduce a noun phrase and specify its meaning. They provide context and detail about the noun they precede, including quantity, possession, or definiteness, as shown in *a student*, *some students*, *my students*, *the student*, *these students*, and so on. Determiners that 'determine' a noun are divided into three subclasses: pre-determiners, central determiners, and post-determiners depending on their relative positions before a noun.

2.5.2 Pre-determiners

Pre-determiners can come before central determiners and provide additional information about the noun. They typically specify quantity or degree. Examples are as follows:

All the students passed the exam. (Pre-determiner: *All*)
Both books were interesting. (Pre-determiner: *Both*)
Such a beautiful day! (Pre-determiner: *Such*)
What a wonderful painting! (Pre-determiner: *What*)

1. *all, half, both*
   All/Half/Both the members agreed to his proposal.
   Both my friends have fallen in love with Jenifer.
   He gave *all* her money back.
   It took *half* an hour to finish cleaning the bathroom.
   Half (of) the food went bad/rotten.
   Half (of) the house was damaged because of the hurricane.
   Half (of) the students attended the meeting.
   I spent *half* my life here.

My brother gave me *half* his salary.
A *half* mile vs. *half* a mile[31]

2. multipliers (numbers by which another number is multiplied): *double*, *twice*, *three times*, *ten times*, etc
My friend was offered *double/twice/ten times* his salary.
Jenifer eats *twice* the normal amount of lunch.

3. fractions (ways of representing parts of a whole): *a-third*, *two-thirds*, *one-fourth*, etc.
They had *one-third/two-thirds/one-fourth* the oil I needed.[32]

4. *what*, *such* (Both of these can function as intensifiers.)
What a wonderful world! (*What* functions as an intensifier.)
It is *such* a beautiful day that we are considering a road trip.
(= … *so* beautiful a day …) (*Such* functions as an intensifier)
I'm glad you had *such* a good journey. (=You had a very good journey)
such terrible weather, (*so …)
The new book offers such interesting ideas about the future of technology.
The BTS Army is glad the concert was such a success. (= … a great success)
such people (that kind of people; a certain type of people with particular traits or qualities), The council is thinking about building a new park. I would support *such* a project. The team plans to change the strategy. I would support *such* a move. ('like this/that,' 'of this/that kind')
such interesting ideas (high degree: 'very,' 'great')

Such has some particular combinations with other determiners as follows:

---

31 Especially, some American writers regard *a half mile* as more formal and correct than *half a mile*.

32 The sentence *They had one-third/two-thirds/one-fourth (of)* the *oil I needed* is grammatically correct in both forms (with or without *of*) (cf. Quirk *et al.* 1985:261).

all (pre-det) *such* necessary stationery: All such necessary stationery was provided for the event.
no (central det) *such* thing/person: No *such* thing exists in our records. There is no (central det) *such* thing as a free ride.
some/any/many (post-det) *such* boys, many such suffixes, several *such* thoughtful gestures, some *such* generous offer, any *such* beautiful painting: *Many such suffixes* are used in English grammar. *Any such beautiful painting* would look great on the wall.

2.5.3 Central determiners

Central determiners are words that typically appear before nouns to specify them. They include articles, demonstratives, and possessives, and interrogatives.

Articles: *the*, *a*, *an*

The car is parked outside.

Demonstratives (indicate or point to specific people, things or entities, often in relation to distance (either physical or metaphorical) from the speaker or listener): *this*, *that*, *these*, *those*

I like *this* car more than *that* one. *This* book is mine. I have read *those* books. *Those* houses were built last year.

Possessives: *my*, *your*, *his*, *her*, *its*, *our*, *their*

Her phone is on the table.
Your old notebook is better than *his* new one.

Interrogatives: *which*, *what*

Which phone do you prefer, Galaxy 24 or iPhone 16?
What time is it?

Relatives: *whose*, *which*, *whatever*, *whichever*

The artist *whose* paintings are in the gallery will give a talk tomorrow.
The man *whose* car was stolen called the police station.
He passed it to Holland, at *which* point Son made a crucial interception.
I will support *whatever* decision you make.
You can take *whatever* dissert you like.
(*Whatever*: Broader and less specific; any dissert within the general category is acceptable; With no emphasis on the limitations or specifics of the options.)
Whichever book you choose, make sure to read it carefully.
Whichever path you take, make sure to follow the directions carefully.
You can choose whichever book you prefer from the collection.
You can take *whichever* brand you prefer from the collection.
Whichever candidate wins the election has to address the issue.
(*Whichever*: Used when you are choosing from defined, mentioned, or known options.)

2.5.4 Post-determiners

The post-determiners follow central determiners and provide additional specification, often related to quantity or identity. They include numerals and quantifiers

Numerals: *one, two, three, …; first, second, third, …; next, last*[33]

He has *three* dogs.
The *first* prize went to John.
I have just read the *first* chapter.
The *two* chapters are about health issues.
I have just read the *first two* chapters.
His *next* film is about environmental issues and climate justice.
Hemingway's *last* major work of fiction is *The Old Man and the Sea.*

33 These are referred to as *general ordinals* (Quirk *et al.* 1985:261).

Quantifiers: *many, few, several; much, little; other*

Many protesters gathered for a rally in Gwanghwamoon.
Politicians should be aware of the *many* economic crises we face.
The *other* students were all prepared for the test, except for me.

Here are some noun phrases with varying numbers of determiners:

Pre-determiner	Central determiner	Post-determiner	Noun
all (quantifier)	*my*	*three*	*songs*
All	*those*		*students*
All	*the*		*options*
All	*his*		*questions*
Both	*our*		*teachers*
Both	*(the)*		*cars*
Twice	*the*		*distance*
Twice	*his*		*age*
Twice	*the*		*price*
Double	*her*		*salary*
Double	*their*		*efforts*
	those	*five*	*cars*
	These	*three*	*books*
	The	*first three*	chapters

Many determiners can also function as pronouns.

All (the students) passed the exam.
Some (people) were happy with the decision.
Many (students) attended the workshop.
Each (person) received a ticket.
Few (employees) attended the meeting.
This (book) is interesting.
That (car) is so fast.
They lost the match, but *such* is life.

In each case, the determiner specifies a noun, while the pronoun replaces the noun phrase, making sentences less repetitive and more concise.

2.5.5 References

Reference refers to the relationship between a noun phrase and the entity or entities it denotes within a given context. In essence, it is about how a noun phrase connects to the actual persons, things, or concepts it represents. The reference of noun phrases can be divided based on genericity, specificity, and definiteness as follows:

- **generic** and **non-generic**
- **specific** and **non-specific**
- **definite** and **non-definite**

These three sets of **references** help explain different ways noun phrases refer to entities.

1. Generic and non-generic reference

Generic reference refers to a type, class, or category of entities as a whole, rather than individual members. A noun phrase is generic when it refers to the entire class, not individual members. In contrast, a noun phrase is non-generic when it refers to individual members of the entire class, rather than the entire class:

Generic reference

Dinosaurs went extinct about 66 million years ago.
The dog has been domesticated for thousands of years.
Dogs became domesticated thousands of years ago.

A/The dog is a faithful animal/man's best friend.
Giraffes are the tallest animals.
Cats are independent animals. generic reference
An ape likes bananas. A Korean is diligent.
Apes like bananas. Koreans are diligent.
The ape likes bananas. The Korean is diligent.
(This can also be read as non-generic.)
The apes like bananas. The Koreans are diligent.
(This can also be read as non-generic.)

An ape and *apes* are generic, referring to any member of the group rather than a specific individual. The distinction lies in how the noun phrases are used to convey generality versus specificity. Tense can influence how we interpret references. For example, present tense often conveys general or habitual truths, as in *A dog barks*, indicating a general characteristic of dogs. In contrast, past tense, like in *A dog barked*, typically refers to a particular/specific event or instance. This can affect whether the reference is seen as generic/non-generic or specific/non-specific. Tense, therefore, plays a crucial role in shaping the meaning and scope of noun phrases in a sentence.

Non-generic reference

Joan got *a dog* from a friend.
I have a plan to give her *the puppies*.
He saw *dogs* running in the park.
The dog is what I like.

2. **Specific** and **non-specific reference**

Specific and non-specific reference refers to the way a noun phrase refers to an entity, such as a person, animal, thing, place, or occurrence. The difference hinges on whether the entity is particular to the speaker or listener at the time of speaking or not. A noun phrase is specific when it refers to a particular entity. In contrast, a noun phrase is non-specific when it refers to any entity within a class or category, not a particular one.

Specific reference

a. *A panda* is eating bamboo, and *two giraffes*, leaves and grass.
b. I saw *a giraffe* in the zoo.
c. They have a plan to send *the panda* to *the zoo.*
d. They sent *a panda* to *the zoo.*

The above noun phrases *a panda* and *two giraffes* in (a), *a giraffe* in (b), *the panda* in (c), and *a panda* and *the zoo* in (d) indicate specific references, since they refer to particular members of those classes.

Non-specific reference

a. I like to ride a horse.
b. I like to read *books/a book.*
c. They have a plan to send *a panda* to the zoo.

The above noun phrases *a horse* in (a), *books/a book* in (b), and *a panda* in (c) are non-specific, since they refer to any members of those classes, not particular ones.

Noun phrases with the indefinite article *a(n)* may be specific or non-specific, depending on contexts, as shown in the relevant examples. In addition, noun phrases of plural forms may be generic or non-generic, depending on contexts, as shown in the relevant examples.

3. Definite and indefinite reference

The **definite article** *the* is used to refer to a specific noun known to both the speaker and the listener or identifiable in context. **Definite reference** identifies a distinct entity assumed to be recognized by both parties as follows:

A. Previously mentioned entities

A: We need to address the budget cuts.
B: I know *the issue* should be discussed soon.
A: I watched a movie last night.
B: How was *the movie*?

B. Entities known to speaker and listener (shared knowledge)

The sun is very important to humans and all living things
The moon affects the tides of the oceans.
The concert was amazing last night.
I can't believe *the concert* last night was so amazing!
The President declared martial law on December 3, 2024.

C. Uniquely identifiable entities (situational context)

Please open *the door*.
Will you pass me *the salt*?
The chair you are sitting on is broken.

D. Definite descriptions identified by modifiers

I'm looking for *the book on the shelf*.
The tall man in the corner is my uncle.
The book on the shelf is what I want to read.

The book written by J.K. Rowling is a bestseller.
The car parked outside is new.

E. Definite descriptions by proper nouns, possessives, and demonstratives

Paris is beautiful in spring.
Her ideas were innovative.
This car is faster than that one.

Indefinite Reference

I need *a pen.*
Any book will do.
A student asked a question.
Someone called while you were out.
Something is bothering him.
An idea came to mind.
A child is playing outside.

Summary of references

<table>
<tr><th colspan="2">Reference</th><th>Example</th></tr>
<tr><td>generic</td><td>non-specific</td><td>Giraffes are the tallest animals
The/A giraffe is the tallest animal.
Cats are independent animals.</td></tr>
<tr><td rowspan="2">non-generic</td><td>specific</td><td>I saw giraffes in the zoo.
I sent the giraffes to the zoo</td></tr>
<tr><td>non-specific</td><td>I like to ride a horse.
I like to read a book/books.</td></tr>
<tr><td colspan="2">specific</td><td>A panda is eating bamboo, and two giraffes, leaves and grass.</td></tr>
<tr><td colspan="2">non-specific</td><td>I like to ride a horse.</td></tr>
<tr><td colspan="2">definite</td><td>the restaurant we visited last week</td></tr>
<tr><td colspan="2">indefinite</td><td>Any book will do. I need a pen</td></tr>
</table>

2.6 Auxiliary verbs

2.6.1 Classes of auxiliary verbs

Auxiliary verbs can be used before the main verb to form various tenses, moods, voices, and aspects of a verb phrase. They are largely classified into two core categories: primary auxiliaries (*be*, *do*, *have*) and modal auxiliaries (will, can, may, shall, must, etc.).[34] In addition to these, there are also non-core auxiliaries (*have to*, *be about to*, *be going to*, *be able to*, *had better*, *ought to*, *used to*, *be to*, etc.).

2.6.2 Primary auxiliaries

1. The progressive auxiliary *be*

   There *are playing* soccer.
   Joan *was studying* in the library.

2. The passive auxiliary *be*

   The apartment *was built* two years ago.
   The town *was devastated* by the tornado.
   My car *was stolen* yesterday.

3. The perfect auxiliary *have*

   They *have finished* the project.
   Samuel *has prepared* for the interview for an hour.

4. Auxiliary *do*

   The auxiliary verb *do* is used to form questions, negatives, and

---

34 These are also called **central modals** (Quirk *et al.* 1985:137).

emphatic statements, reflecting tense, person, and number. The base form of the main verb is used after the auxiliary *do*.

Did you go to the BTS concert last night?
I *do* not understand what you are talking about.
I *do* want to go.
I *did* finish the work.
I believe Joan *did* vote for Kate.

2.6.3. Modal auxiliaries[35]

Modal auxiliaries, except for *must*, have distinctions between present and past tense as follows:

Present/past *will/would, can/could, may/might, shall/should, must*

However, their past forms can also express present or future time. Modals can express various meanings such as future, intention, ability, possibility, obligation, permission, necessity, etc. as follows:

1. will/would

I *will* call you tomorrow. (future actions or intention)
I *would* go if I were you. (a hypothetical situation)

---

35 Central modals, marginal modals, modal idioms, semi-auxiliaries, and catenatives are types of verbs that express modality, functioning along a continuum between main verbs and modal verbs. "Central modals (will, can, may, etc), marginal modals (dare, need, ought to, used to), modal idioms (had better, would rather/sooner, be to, have got to, etc.), semi-auxiliaries (have to, be about/able/bound/going/ obliged/supposed/willing to, etc.), catenatives (appear to, happen to, seem to, get + -*ed* participle, keep + -*ing* participle, etc.), main verb + nonfinite clause (hope + *to*-infinitive, begin + -*ing* participle)" (Quirk *et al.* 1985:137).

Would you do me a favor? (a polite request)
Would you like some coffee or tea? (a polite offer)
I *would* go fishing every weekend. (only repeated actions in the past)

2. can/could

She *can* speak two languages, English and Spanish. (ability)
You *can* find a good restaurant in this area. (possibility)
When I was younger, I *could* swim across the river. (past ability)
Could you help me with this report? (a polite request)
He *could* be at the office now. (present possibility)
It *could* rain later today. (future possibility)
We *could* go on vacation next month if we save enough money.

3. may/might

May/Could/*Can* I leave early tomorrow? (asking for permission)
You *may* start the test when you're ready. (granting permission)
We *may* go to the park tomorrow if it's sunny. (future possibility)
He *may* know the answer to your question. (present possibility)
I *might* go to the party. (low probability or uncertainty)
Might I ask you a question? (a polite permission, especially in BE)

4. must

You *must* fasten your seatbelt in the car. (obligation)
You *must* bring your ID to the airport for security checks. (obligation)
You *must* wash your hands before preparing food. (necessity)
You *must* try the new restaurant downtown. (strong recommendation)
She's not here; she *must* be at work. (a strong belief or certainty)

5. shall/should

Shall we dance? *Shall* we go for a walk? (offers or suggestions)
The tenant *shall* pay the rent on the first of every month.
(a requirement or obligation, especially in legal or formal contexts)

You *should* see a doctor if the pain persists. (advice)
You *should* be considerate to others. (moral obligation)
You *should* definitely try the lasagna at that restaurant.
(A strong recommendation)
In many cultures, people *should* greet each other with a handshake.
Korea *should* win this match. She *should* be home by now. (expectation)

2.6.4. Non-core auxiliaries

Non-core auxiliary verbs function similarly to modal verbs but are not considered true modals. They include *have to*, *be about to*, *be going to*, *be able to*, *had better*, *ought to*, *used to*, *be to*, etc.

1. have (got) to

I *have (got) to* finish this work. (obligation)
I *have (got) to* be back by tomorrow. (obligation)
My kids usually *have to* go to bed before 10 p.m.
*My kids *have usually got to* go to bed before 10 p.m.
(not used for habitual or repeated obligations)
You *have got to* be kidding me! (certainty)
This *has got to* be the best movie I've ever seen! (certainty)
That guy *has to* be the one who broke the window. (certainty)
Ought to: Indicates advice or duty (e.g., You ought to apologize).

2. have to vs. must

Have to: Reflects an external obligation based on rules, policies, or requirements that are imposed by others (such as hospital policy or legal regulations). It tends to be more neutral and can sound more like a routine requirement.

You *have to* wear a mask in hospitals during this COVID-19 period.
(obligation based on external factors like hospital policy)

Must: Used to express an internal obligation based on personal judgment, moral responsibility, or a sense of urgency about a situation.

You *must* wear a mask in hospitals during this COVID-19 period.
(Judgment on infection or safety, an internal or moral obligation)

3. be about to: Something is going to happen very soon.

The conference *is about to* start.

4. be going to: future arrangements/plans, intentions, or predictions based on current evidence. (cf. will: spontaneous decisions)

I'*m going to* visit my grandparents next weekend.
It'*s going to* rain soon.

5. be able to: ability to do something in the present, past, or future in specific situations.

I *am able to* speak two languages. (= I have the ability to speak ...)
He will *be able to* help you tomorrow.
She *was able to (*could)* solve the math problem during the exam. (*was able to* for specific actions or achievements in the past; *could* for general abilities or repeated actions: She *could* always solve math problems)

6. had better: advice or a strong recommendation

You *had better* study for the exam.
We *had better* leave soon if we want to catch the train.

7. ought to: advice, duty or moral obligation, or the right thing to do

He *ought to* be more careful. (advice)
We *ought to* help those in need. (a moral obligation to help)

You *ought to* apologize for what you said. (suggest the right thing)

8. used to: past habits, actions, or states that no longer occur. (cf. would)

I *used to* go jogging every morning. = In the past, I had the habit of jogging every morning, but I no longer do.
They *used to (*would)* live in New York. = In the past, they lived in New York, but they don't anymore.

9. be to+infinitive

This structure is used to express the following meanings:

A. a scheduled or planned event

The conference *is to* start at 1 p.m.
(=The conference *is scheduled/planned to* start at 1 p.m.)
The President *is to* visit France next month.
(=The President *is scheduled/planned to* visit …)

B. an obligation or requirement

They *are to* report to the mayor immediately in case of emergency.
(=They *must/are required to* report …)
The project *is to* be completed by Friday.
(=The project *must/is required to* be completed by Friday.)
You *are to* follow all safety procedures while working.
(=You *must/are required to* follow …)

C. destiny or fate

He *was to* marry Joan. (=He *was destined to* marry Joan)

D. possibility or potentiality

Nobody *was to* be seen. (=Nobody *could* be seen)

E. a prohibition or restriction (something not allowed)

Visitors *are not to* enter the building without permission.
(=Visitors *are not allowed to* enter …)

F. intention or purpose

If you *are to* succeed, you must work harder.
(=If you *intend to* succeed, you must work harder.)

2.7 Adjectives

Adjectives generally modify or characterize nouns to describe qualities or states as in *She has a beautiful house* and *The house is beautiful*. They can be identified based on their suffixes.

2.7.1 Adjective suffixes

Here are some common examples:

-ful: *beautiful, careful, joyful, painful, respectful, skillful, thoughtful*
-less: *careless, endless, fearless, helpless, hopeless, motionless*
-able/-ible: *breakable, comfortable, plausible, responsible, sensible*
-ic: *artistic, dramatic, economic, historic, public, romantic, symbolic*
-ical: *chemical, critical, historical, logical, mathematical, theoretical*
-ous/-ious/-eous: *dangerous, famous, mysterious, righteous*
-al/-ial: *combinational, emotional, financial, inferential, official*
-ive, -ative: *active, alternative, creative, destructive, talkative*
-ed: *bored, closed, embarrassed, excited, interested, tensed, tired*
-ed: *blue-eyed, good-natured, long-haired, one-legged, open-minded*
-y: *cloudy, greasy, greedy, messy, rainy, shiny, sticky, spicy, sunny*
-ary: , *customary, imaginary, legendary, revolutionary, secretary*
-an/-ian: *American, Asian, Indian, Korean, Mexican, musician*

-ish: *boyish, childish, foolish, greenish, reddish, selfish, Spanish*
-like: *childlike, finlike, godlike, manlike, lifelike, womanlike*
-ent: *dependent, different, insistent, persistent, prevalent*
-ant: *elegant, important, malignant, resistant, significant*

The suffixes are added to nouns or verbs to form adjectives, which describe attributes, qualities, or relations related to the nouns they modify.

2.7.2 Functions of adjectives

1. Functions of adjectives

There are three functions of adjectives: pre-modifier, subject complement, and object complement. These functions are illustrated below.

A. **Pre-modifier**: *valuable comments* (The adjective *valuable* comes before the noun it modifies, providing additional information about the noun.)

B. **Subject complement**: *My work experience in Seattle is valuable.* (The adjective *valuable* follows a linking verb and describes the subject.)

C. **Object complement**: *I consider my work experience valuable.* (The adjective *valuable* follows the direct object and characterizes it.)

2. Uses of adjectives

Adjectives can also be categorized based on how they are used in sentences. Some adjectives can function as pre-modifier, subject complement, and object complement, and are often called **central adjectives**. Examples include *valuable*, *good*, *famous*, *wise*, *wonderful*, etc.

In contrast, there are adjectives that can be used only as pre-modifiers or only as complements.[36] These adjectives are typically restricted to one use: either attributive use (as pre-modifiers) or predicative use (as complements).

A. Attributive use only: Adjectives used only as pre-modifiers (e.g., *main roads*). These adjectives (e.g., *chief*, *elder*, *former*, *latter*, *main*, *major*, *primary*, *principal*, *sheer*, *ultimate*, *utter*, *very*) cannot function as subject or object complements.

B. Predicative use only: Adjectives that appear only in the complement position (e.g., *The baby is asleep*, *I found him asleep*). These adjectives (e.g., *afloat*, *afraid*, *alike*, *alive*, *alone*, *awake*, *(un)aware*, *content*, *loath*, *subject*) cannot function as pre-modifiers.

Some predicative adjectives require a post-modifier to complete their meanings as follows:

Steve was *aware* of the risks involved in the decision.
He is *inclined* to listen to others' opinions.
He was *loath* to make a speech before the large audience.
He was *oblivious* to the risks in his investment.
They are *subject* to the new health and safety regulations.

The attributive or predicative use of some adjectives depends on their meanings.

He is *fond* of cooking/pets. (having a liking for: **predicative use only**)
Steve gave Joan a *fond* look. (loving: **attributive use only**)

---

36 These adjectives are called **peripheral adjectives** or **non-central adjectives**. (cf. Quirk *et al*. 1985:404)

Tom nourished *fond* hopes of becoming president.
(foolishly optimistic: **attributive use only**)
He invested in the start-up in the *fond* hope that it would pay off.
(foolishly trusting: **attributive use only**)

In addition to attributive use and predicative use, adjectives can also have a **postpositive use**, where they come after the noun they modify.

C. Postpositive use: Adjectives that appear immediately after the noun they modify, rather than before it. Postpositive adjectives are less common than prepositive adjectives (those placed before the noun), but they can still be quite effective in certain contexts.

- **Indefinite pronouns/adverbs (*-body*, *-one*, *-thing*, *-where*) with postpositive adjectives**

Find *something valuable* in your experience.
We need *someone reliable* to handle it during my absence.
Nothing impossible stands in our way if we work together.
Do you have *anything useful* that could help with my research?
Let's go *somewhere nice.*

- **Fixed expressions** (French influence on word order)

attorney *general*, court *martial*, heir *apparent*, notary *public*, poet *laureate*, the president-*elect*, from/since time *immemorial*

- **Other uses of postpositive adjectives**

He does not live in Boston *proper.*
The interviewers have a friendly chat before the interview *proper* to relax the candidate.

- **Both postpositive and prepositive uses**
  the best candidate *possible* (= the best *possible* candidate)
  the best actor *available* (= the best *available* actor)
  In years *past* (= in *past* years)

2.7.3 Comparison

Adjectives allow for varying degrees of description and comparison between nouns. They can express different levels of a quality, known as gradability. For instance, *smart* can vary in degree or intensity:

- Same degree describes qualities that are equal in level between two items: *Jane is as smart as her sister.*
- Higher Degree indicates a greater level of a quality in one item compared to another or others: *Jane is smarter than her sister* (comparative) and *Jane is the smartest of her siblings* (superlative).
- Lower Degree suggests a lesser level of a quality in one item compared to another or others: *Jane is less smart than her sister* and *Jane is the least smart student in the class.*

These degrees help express relative comparisons of qualities. Gradable adjectives often take modifiers (or intensifiers) like *a little*, *somewhat*, *quite*, or *very* to indicate varying levels, as in *quite tall*, *very tall*, and *somewhat tired.*

Adjectives can compare the qualities of different nouns. There is a three-term contrast in comparison forms of adjectives.

- **Absolute Form**: *small*
- **Comparative Form**: *smaller*
- **Superlative Form**: *smartest*

Comparative and **superlative forms** of adjectives are represented by inflections (*-er*, *-est*) or pre-modifiers/periphrases (*more*, *most*), depending generally on the number of syllables.

	Absolute	Comparative	Superlative
inflection	big happy polite	bigger happier politer	biggest happiest politest
pre-modifiers/periphrases	polite	more polite	most polite

One-syllable adjectives normally take inflectional endings in their comparative forms and superlative forms. However, there are some exceptions, such as *right*, *wrong*, *real*, and *like*, which more commonly take *more* and *most* instead of inflectional endings.

Her style is *more like* her mother's.
Your explanation is *more right* than mine.

Some two-syllable adjectives have *-er* and *-est* (*clever*, *happy*, *narrow*, *quiet*, *simple*, etc.); others have *more* and *most* (especially, adjectives ending in *-ing*, *-ed*, *-ful*, and *-less*: *boring*, *wicked*, *careful*, *useless*, etc. Some two-syllable adjectives (*polite*, *gentle*, and *common*) can be used with either *-er/-est* or *more/most.*

For adjectives with three or more syllables, the comparative and superlative forms are typically formed using *more* and *most* as in *more beautiful*, *most beautiful.*

Some very common adjectives have irregular comparative and superlative forms as follows:

Irregular comparative and superlative forms

Absolute	Comparative	Superlative
good bad far	better worse farther/further	best worst farthest/furthest
old	elder	eldest

This book is *better* than the last one.
She is the *best* student in the class.
The weather today is *worse* than yesterday.
This is the *worst* day of the year.
The store is *farther* from my house than the gym.
This research is *further* along than expected.
The moon is the *farthest* object visible in the sky.
He went the *furthest* in the competition.
Her *elder*/*eldest* son is a teacher.

Adjectives like *circular*, *complete*, *entire*, *excellent*, *perfect*, and *unique* typically do not take comparative or superlative forms, as their meaning does not allow for a degree of comparison. However, in some contexts, comparative or superlative forms of these words can still be found, often due to contextual or stylistic reasons. The same applies to their adverb counterparts, such as *circularly*, *completely*, *entirely*, *excellently*, *perfectly*, and *uniquely*.

2.7.4 Major usage of comparison

1. Comparison of two qualities of the same entity

When we compare two different characteristics of the same entity (like a person or thing), we generally use the comparative form with *more* instead of the *-er* suffix, even when the adjectives in question are one-syllable or two-syllable words.

He is *more clever* (*cleverer) than wise.
Her explanation was *more clear* (*clearer) than vague.

2. Use of *most* for emphasis (not superlative-forming)

The word *most* can be used to mean the intensifier *very*, but not superlative-forming word as follows:

That is *most* (=very) kind of you.
That is *most* generous of you.
She is *most* kind and caring.
It was *most* considerate of him to help us.

2.8 Adverbs

2.8.1 Adverb suffixes

Adverbs function as modifiers in phrases or as adverbials in clauses, as in *very cute* and *They are singing beautifully*. Adverb suffixes are added to adjectives or other base words to form adverbs. These adverbs can often be identified by their suffixes.

1. The most common adverb suffix *-ly* is added to adjectives to form adverbs, very often indicating the manner in which an action is performed.

   She ran *quickly*.
   They lived *happily* ever after.

He handled the glass *carefully.*

Adjectives that end in *-ic* typically take the suffix *-ically.*

dramatically, economically, geologically, heroically, historically, phonetically, politically, romantically

2. The suffix *-wise* often indicates manner or direction, which is less common than *-ly*. It can be added to nouns or adjectives to form adverbs.

The hands of the clock move *clockwise.*
Turn the knob *anticlockwise* to loosen it.
You should study hard; *otherwise*, you may fail the test.

3. The suffix *-ward(s)* form adverbs that describe the direction in which something moves.

The car moved *forward.*
Stock prices move *upward* or *downward* over time.

4. The suffix *-fold* is used to indicate multiplication or increase in number or degree.

The company's revenue increased *twofold* after the product launch.
His investment has increased *twofold.*

There are many adverbs without any suffixes.

- **time adverbs**: *later, now, soon, then, today, tomorrow, yesterday*
- **place adverbs**: *here, there, inside, outside, anywhere, somewhere*
- **frequency adverbs**: *sometimes, often, always, seldom, never*
- **degree adverbs**: *enough, quite, so, too, very*[37]

37 These are also called **intensifiers**.

- **manner adverbs**: *fast*, *hard*, *high*, *late*, *straight*, *well*

2.8.2 Functions of adverbs

1. Adverbs function as modifiers in phrases.

The chemical is *incredibly* addictive.
The service in the restaurant is *quite* good.
They made a decision *quite* reasonably.
They are preparing *really* hard for the test.

2. Adverbs function as adverbials in clauses.

She arrived in London *early*.
I finished the project *yesterday*.
They are singing *beautifully*.

2.8.3 Comparison

Adverbs, like adjectives, can also be gradable and express varying degrees of manner, time, frequency, and so on. Adverbs can be modified by **intensifiers** such as *a little*, *quite*, *so*, *very*, or *totally* as in *a little/quite/very/totally differently*. Some adverbs describe actions or conditions that are considered absolute or not subject to varying degrees. These adverbs are typically not modified with intensifiers as in **very never* and **very always*.

Adverbs can be used in comparative and superlative forms as follows:

Jennifer can speak Spanish *as fluently as* Joan.
Jennifer speaks Spanish *more fluently than* Joan.
Jennifer speaks Spanish *most fluently* in the class.
She woke up *earlier* than usual.

Some very common adverbs have irregular comparative and superlative forms as follows:

Irregular comparative and superlative forms

Absolute	Comparative	Superlative
much	more	most
well	better	best
badly	worse	worst
far	farther/further	farthest/furthest
little	less	least

2.9 Prepositions

Prepositions connect nouns, pronouns, or phrases to other parts in a sentence, specifying relationships of direction, location, time, manner, and more. A preposition must be followed by its complement (e.g., *in the room*). There are many prepositions, as shown in the following examples:

- **Direction (movement)**

  Steve went *to* the library.
  Steve ran *into* the house.
  Steve ran *out of* the house.
  Steve walked *toward(s)* the tower.
  Yonsei University is *to* the north of the Han River. (direction)
  This express bus is bound *for* Busan. (destination)

- **Location/place**

  Kate is *at* Stanford/the station/the library/the theater.
  (specific place/point; small places)

Steve lives *in* Seoul/New York/Paris/Korea. (larger places)
Steve lay *on* the floor. (surface)
Jennifer lives *at* 25 King Street. (specific address/point)
Jennifer lives *on* Seventh Street. (streets, roads, or specific surfaces)
William walked along the country road just *off* the main freeway.
Steve saw a cat *out of* the window.
The flower pot stood *in* the corner of the living room.
(*corner* is a three-dimensional space)

- **Location and movement/direction**: along, across

Many stores stand *along* the street. (location)
Joan took a walk *along* the lake. (movement/direction)
The NH bank is right *across* the street. (location)
The ferry sailed *across* the ocean. (movement/direction)

- **Prepositions of place**: over/under, above/below

There is a long bridge *over* the lake.
The cat is sleeping *under* the bed.
Look at the painting *on* the wall.
The treasure was buried *beneath* the old oak tree.
An old castle is located *above* the valley.
The basement is *below* the ground floor.

- **Prepositions of time**: at, on, in, by

Steve will arrive *at* 10 AM/noon. (specific points in time)
Steve left the house *at* dawn. (specific moments of the day)
Her birthday is *on* April 7th. (specific dates)
We will meet *on* Friday. (days of the week)
The party is *on* Christmas Eve. (specific holidays or days)
Daniel was born *in* 1997. (specific years)
I will finish the project *in* March. (specific months)

Jennifer will visit us *in* the winter. (seasons)
She will finish the work *in* a week. (time frames for completion)
for an hour/ten days/three months/ten years (duration)
during my stay in Boston/my absence. (specific period)
He will stay here *until/*by* March 7. (continuation up to that time)
He will arrive here **until/by* March 7. (not later than)
Please submit your application *by* June 5. (deadline)
I met Bill (**on*) *last* Monday.
Apples are plentiful (**in*) *this* year.
Next year, Sam will go to graduate school.
Every winter we make a trip to Hawaii.

• **Other prepositions**

Steve wrote *with* a pen. (manner)
He traveled *by* bus. (mode of transportation)
I'm paid *by* the hour. (measurement)
She's taller than her sister *by* two inches.
(measurement of difference)
The book was written *by* Mark Twain. (agency)

• **Complex prepositions** consist of more than one word. They often combine a simple preposition with another word to convey more specific or nuanced meanings.

I usually park my car *in front of* the house.
She sat *next to* him at the table.
The book is *on top of* the shelf.
The flight was canceled *due to/owing to/because of* bad weather.
Because of/Owing to her illness, she couldn't attend the conference.
He completed the race *in spite of* his injury.
In case of an emergency, call 911.
The package was delivered *by means of* courier.

I have some questions *with regard to* the new policy.
With regard to/With respect to/In regard to/Regarding/As to/Concerning the issue, you can ask your consultant.

2.10 Conjunctions

Conjunctions connect words, phrases, or clauses within a sentence, helping to establish relationships and link ideas. They play an important role in forming multiple sentences and making communication coherent and clear. Conjunctions can be categorized into several types based on their function:

2.10.1 Coordinating conjunctions (Coordinators)

Coordinating conjunctions connect two or more words, phrases, or independent clauses that are of equal grammatical rank or status in a sentence, and include *and*, *or*, and *but*.

- **And**

I bought apples, pears, *and* oranges.
We planned to visit the museum *and* see a movie.
The sun was shining brightly, *and* the birds were singing melodiously.
Manage your time efficiently, *and* you will succeed.

- **Or**

Manage your time efficiently, *or* you will not succeed.
I didn't decide whether to call her *or* send an email.
You can stay home and rest *or* go out and enjoy the evening.
Would you like tea *or* coffee?

- **But**

The dress was beautiful *but* expensive.
The room was quiet *but* dark.
I wanted to go to the park, *but* it started raining.
Their plan was not to relax on vacation *but* to explore new cities.

2.10.2 Subordinating conjunctions (Subordinators)

Subordinating conjunctions connect a subordinate clause to a main clause (also called a superordinate clause), showing their relationship. The subordinate clause relies on the main clause to form a meaningful statement.

Subordinating conjunctions often indicate the relationship between the clauses, such as:

- **Time**: after, before, since, until, when(ever), while, as soon as

After the conference ended, we went for dinner.
As soon as the sun set, the temperature dropped dramatically here.

- **Place**: where, wherever

He will go *where* his brothers go.
Wherever you go, I will follow you.

- **Cause and effect**: as, because, since, in that

As it was raining, he stayed home.
I didn't go to the party *because* I was tired.

- **Concession**: although, though

Although it was cold, we went for a walk.
Though Jennifer tried hard, she couldn't finish the project on time.

- **Contrast**: whereas, while

  She likes to work in the morning, *whereas* he works late at night.
  While Suzan is good at arts, her brothers are good at sports.

- **Condition**: if, unless

  If it rains tomorrow, we'll cancel the picnic.
  Unless something unexpected occurs, the project will go on.

- **Others**: that, whether

  I didn't realize *that* you had difficulty finishing the project.
  She didn't decide *whether* to attend the conference.

** Use of *Whether* vs. *If* (Huddleston and Pullum 2002:973-974)

• The exclusive use of *whether*

1. Exhaustive Conditional Clauses
I'm going to finish this research *whether*/**if* you help me *or not.*

2. Infinitival Clauses

She didn't decide *whether*/**if to attend* the conference.

3. When the subordinate clause occurs sentence-initially

[*Whether*/**If* they will accept the offer]$_S$ is still unknown.
[*Whether*/**If* he will win the race]$_{DO}$, we'll know soon.

4. When the subordinator is immediately followed by *or not*

We don't know *whether*/**if or not* they'll accept our offer.

(However, when *or not* is part of a coordinated structure, both *whether* and *if* are acceptable.)
We don't know *whether/if* they'll accept our offer (*or not*).

5. When *whether* is used as a complement to the verb be or as a supplement to a noun phrase

The current question *is* [*whether*/**if* they will solve the problems]$_{SC}$.
This question, [*whether*/**if* he violated the Constitution and Martial Law Act]$_{\text{appositive clause}}$, must be carefully investigated.

6. When the relevant clause follows a preposition

It depends *on* [*whether*/**if* we have enough time left]$_{PC}$.

2.10.3 Correlative conjunctions

Correlative conjunctions are pairs of conjunctions that work together to join units of equal status such as words, phrases, or clauses.

- **Both...and**: *Both* Tom *and* Jane go to the party.
- **Either...or**: You can *either* go shopping *or* stay home.
- **Neither...nor**: Steve wants *neither* coffee *nor* tea.
- **Not only...but also**: He is *not only* talented *but also* hardworking.

2.10.4 Conjunctive adverbs

Conjunctive adverbs act as conjunctions to typically connect independent clauses (or sometimes sentences), often showing relationships like contrast, cause and effect, or addition. They are also used with a semicolon.

- **However**: I wanted to go; *however*, it was too late.

- **Therefore**: She studied hard; *therefore*, she passed the exam.
- **Moreover**: The proposal was sound; *moreover*, it was cost-effective.
- **Thus**: Typically, *thus* is used to show a direct cause-and-effect relationship, and it usually comes after a semicolon or at the beginning of a new sentence.

He was tired; thus, he went to bed early.
He was tired. Thus, he went to bed early.

Exercises

1. Identify whether the *italicized* genitives are dependent or independent.

   (1) *The company's* profits increased significantly, but *its competitors'* did not.
   (2) *Sarah's* decision was final, despite *her parents'* concerns.
   (3) *The professor's* lecture was insightful, but *the graduate student's* was difficult to follow.
   (4) We visited *the artist's* studio and admired her paintings, but *the gallery's* collection was even more impressive.

2. Identify whether the *italicized* parts are possessive determiners or possessive pronouns.

   (1) Is this *your* notebook or *mine*?
   (2) She lost *her* phone, but luckily, I found *hers*.
   (3) We need to submit *our* project before they submit *theirs*.
   (4) I borrowed *his* jacket because I forgot *mine* at home.
   (5) They sold *their* house and moved into *ours*.

3. Fill in each blank with the appropriate reflexive pronoun.

   (1) She blamed _________ for the mistake.
   (2) The children made lunch for _________ while their parents were away.
   (3) I hurt _________ while lifting heavy boxes.

(4) We found ________ lost in the unfamiliar city.
(5) You should be proud of ________ for completing the project.

4. Identify whether the *italicized* part is a demonstrative pronoun or a demonstrative determiner.

(1) *That* is exactly what I was looking for.
(2) I like *those* shoes; they look comfortable.
(3) *This* is the best concert I've ever attended.
(4) Could you pass me *those* books from the top shelf?
(5) *Those* are the stories I love to tell.

5. Identify whether the *italicized* clause is a relative clause or a nominal relative clause.

(1) They hired *whoever was most qualified for the position.*
(2) The book *that she recommended* was very informative.
(3) You may choose *whichever option fits you best.*
(4) The restaurant *where we had lunch* was excellent.
(5) She will do *whatever is needed* to succeed.

6. Identify whether the *italicized* phrases are generic or non-generic.

(1) *Dogs* are loyal animals.
(2) *The notebook on the table* belongs to Joan.
(3) *A smartphone* can be a useful device for learning.
(4) *The sun* rises in the east.
(5) *That restaurant* serves excellent pasta.

Chapter 3

The Structures of Phrases

Objectives

- To understand the types of phrase structure
- To identify their characteristics and functions

Key words

head, noun phrases, verb phrases, adjective phrases, adverb phrases, prepositional phrases, finite/non-finite verb, tense, aspect, voice, mood

A sentence has a structure with a specific word order, and it consists of various constituents (i.e., units). For example:

A brave firefighter	has rescued	a citizen	in a very dramatic manner.
A	B	C	D

In this sentence, we can identify four main units (A, B, C, D).

A is the subject noun phrase (*A brave firefighter*),
B is the verb phrase (*has rescued*),
C is the object noun phrase (*a citizen*),
D is the adverbial prepositional phrase (*in a very dramatic manner*), which contains an adjective phrase (*very dramatic*).

Each of these phrases has a specific word order, and changing the order would make the sentence ungrammatical, as in **brave a firefighter*, **firefighter a brave*, *a *firefighter brave*, **saved has*,

**citizen a*, **in very a dramatic manner.*

Each phrase is named after its head word (the main word). A **phrase** is a group of words that functions as a single meaningful unit within a sentence. Although phrases usually consist of multiple words, a single word can also function as a phrase if it serves a grammatical role. Unlike a clause, a phrase does not contain both a subject and a predicate. Instead, it typically consists of a main word (the head) and any words that modify or complement it.

Phrases can be classified based on their head and function in a sentence. Common types include noun phrases, verb phrases, adjective phrases, adverb phrases, and prepositional phrases.

- **noun phrase**: the beautiful *mountain*$_{\text{HEAD}}$
- **verb phrase**: will have *dried*$_{\text{HEAD}}$
- **adjective phrase**: very *happy*$_{\text{HEAD}}$
- **adverb phrase**: quite *easily*$_{\text{HEAD}}$
- **prepositional phrase**: *in*$_{\text{HEAD}}$ the classroom

Phrases can include another phrase or a clause as follows:

- a [*very brave*]$_{\text{AP}}$ citizen
- the couple [*who were walking along the lake*]$_{\text{CL}}$

3.1 Noun phrases (NP)

A **noun phrase** is a group of words that functions as a subject, object, or complement in a sentence. It typically consists of a noun or pronoun (the main word or head) and can include other words or groups of words that modify or complement the noun. These additional words can be determiners, adjective phrases, prepositional phrases, or even clauses. These elements work together to provide more detail or clarify the meaning of the noun.

3.1.1 Structure of the noun phrase

A noun phrase typically includes the main word called a **head**, which is a noun or a pronoun, and optionally its determiners and modifiers, as shown in the following:

(determiners)	(pre-modifiers)	noun	(post-modifiers)
the	*expensive*	*car*	*(that) I bought*
	very interesting	*topics*	
	intriguing	*questions*	about the issue
many		*students*	
		something	*special*
	poor	*you*[38]	
	poor old	*Jackie*	
	lucky	*me*	

38 In informal expressions, the second-person pronoun *you* can be modified by adjectives like *poor*, *clever*, or *lucky*, as in *Poor (old) you!* (This sometimes applies to *me* as well, as in *Lucky me*) (Swan 2005:405). *Poor old* (*somebody/ something*) is used to express sympathy (The Free Dictionary).

3.1.2 Determiners

As mentioned in the previous chapter, we have three subclasses of determiners

- pre-determiners: *all*, *each* , *both*, *half*, etc.
- central determiners: *a(n)*, *the*, *this*, *these*, etc.
- post-determiners: *three*, *second*, *last*, *next*, etc.

The following sentences include these determiners.

All the ten books on the table belong to Taylor.
Both our two sons are coming to the event.
The last two chapters are on environmental issues.

3.1.3 Modifiers

In noun phrases, modifiers can be phrases or clauses that provide additional information about the head noun. They enhance the meaning of the noun by describing, identifying, or qualifying it.

- **Pre-modifiers**: They describe characteristics or qualities of the head noun.

The *very bright* sun warmed the garden. (pre-modifier)
She wore a *red* dress. (pre-modifier)
A *beautiful old* house (two pre-modifiers)
Unusual tropical nights lasted for thirty days. (two pre-modifiers)
A long, meandering river (two pre-modifiers)
The company faced *unexpectedly increased* demand for its new product. (pre-modifier)

- **Order of pre-modifiers (adjectives)**

In English, the order of adjectives (pre-modifiers) typically follows a general tendency where more subjective or opinion-based adjectives come earlier in the sequence, while more objective or factual adjectives come later and closer to the noun:

opinion/evaluation, property, size, age, shape, color, participle, origin/style, material, (purpose), noun modifier, adjective from noun, and then the noun.

Opinion/Evaluation (beautiful, lovely)
Size (large, tiny, huge)
Property (soft, smooth, expensive, expensive)
Age (old, new, ancient)
Shape (round, square)
Color (red, blue)
Participles (exciting, broken)
Origin/Style (French, Victorian)
Material (wooden, cotton)
Purpose/Qualifier (dining, sleeping)
Noun modifier (sports, driving)
Noun (the head noun)

A beautiful large soft old round wooden dining table.
(opinion-size-property-age-shape-material-purpose/qualifier-Noun)
A big Italian silk carpet.
A large vintage Italian wool carpet.
A big woven Italian carpet.

- **Post-modifiers**: Post-modifying phrases/clauses are typically relative clauses, *-ing*/*-ed* (participle) clause, prepositional phrases, or adjective phrases.

The car *that he bought last month* is undergoing a few problems.
The person *who called you* is waiting in the office.

The old castle *standing on the hill* is abandoned.
Suzan wore a dress *made of silk.*
The book *with the green cover* is on the top shelf.
This audio system is a gift *for my parents who love music.*

He was wearing a jacket *too big for him.*
The article deals with those *afraid of clustered holes or bumps.*

There are some more examples which include both pre-and post-modifiers.

The *large* building *on the corner* is for sale.
Joan bought a *beautiful old* mansion *on the hill.*

The *beautiful* woman *with the long, flowing dress who is just walking down the red carpet* is a famous actress.

3.1.4 Relative clauses

Relative clauses, also known as modifier clauses, are a type of subordinate clause that modifies an antecedent (a noun or pronoun) in the main clause. They are used to provide additional information about its antecedent (a noun or pronoun) in a sentence.[39]

---

39 The nominal relative pronoun *what* indicates 'the thing(s) which,' meaning it contains an implicit antecedent, i.e., there is no visible antecedent, which is called a **free relative**. The relative clause is therefore a nominal clause. The clause that introduces the relative adverb ***how*** is typically a type of relative clause called a **free relative clause** or **nominal relative clause**. In this case, the clause acts as a noun and typically provides information about the manner or way in which something is done. *She explained **how***

The student *who/that* arrived late is still in the hall.
The officer (*whom/who*) he spoke to was very kind.
The officer to *whom/*who* he spoke was very kind.
The man *whose* car was stolen reported it to the police.
The book *which/that* is on the table is for you.
The car (*which/that*) I bought yesterday is very expensive.
The house *where we grew up* has been renovated since last month.
Hawaii was the place *where we spent our holidays*.
I remember the day *when we met*.
The reason *why she left early* was to take care of her sons.

- **Uses of Relative Clauses**

1. **Restrictive Relative Clauses**: Typically provide essential information that is necessary to specify or identify the antecedent they modify. These clauses are not separated by commas as follows:

   The students *who studied very hard* passed the test
   The car *that broke down* was sent to the service center.

2. **Non-restrictive Relative Clauses**: Provide additional, non-essential information about the antecedent. These clauses are separated by commas as follows:

   My parents, *who live in Seoul*, are visiting me next week.
   Prof. Johnson, who teaches physics, attended the conference last week.

---

she solved the problem. Instead of *how*, *the way* can be used, as in *She explained* ***the way*** <u>*she solved the problem*</u>. The underlined part acts as a post-modifier.

3.1.5 Appositive clauses

An **appositive clause** (*that*-clause, *whether*-clause, and *to* infinitive clause) can be embedded in a noun phrase as follows:

His parents were delighted by [the fact *that he passed the exam*]$_{NP}$.
(The fact is *that he passed the exam*; *that* is an appositive conjunction)
[The idea *that teamwork is very important*]$_{NP}$ is shared by many.
I agree with [his belief *that hard work is the key to success*]$_{NP}$.
He did not fulfill [his duty *to attend the court hearing*]$_{NP}$.
(His duty is *to attend the court hearing*)
[The question *whether climate justice will be realized*]$_{NP}$ is uncertain.
The paper raises [the question *whether they are interrelated*] $_{NP}$.
[The news *that he declared martial law*]$_{NP}$ came as a shock to people.
They agreed with [his explanation *that it was the primary cause of the accident*]$_{NP}$.
[The legend *that a treasure lies buried beneath the tree*]$_{NP}$ has interested many adventurers.

These appositive clauses explain or add information about a noun in the main clause, usually the one immediately preceding them. The appositive clause *that he passed the exam* in one of the above examples adds or explains the information about the noun *fact*.

The conjunction *that* in appositive clauses introduces a complete noun clause (a whole thought), whereas *that* in relative clauses introduces a modifier clause that does not stand as a complete thought on its own, as in the following:

The fact *that* he was guilty shocked him. (subordinating conjunction)
(He was guilty.)
The fact *that* he talked about was very shocking. (relative pronoun)
(*He talked about.)

3.1.6 Apposition

Apposition is a grammatical relationship or construction in which two elements (typically noun phrases) are placed alongside, with one element providing additional information about the other. The noun phrase that follows is in apposition to the first noun phrase and provides additional information about it.

Rome, *the capital of Italia*, is known for its fascinating history.
(Rome is the capital of Italia.)
North Korea developed an ICBM, *an intercontinental ballistic missile.*
The author of *1984*, *George Orwell*, was an influential figure.
Albert Einstein, *the famous physicist*, developed the theory of relativity.

Apposition is sometimes marked by expressions such as *i.e.*, *namely*, *that is* (*to say*), and *or*.

Joan is allergic to certain foods, *namely* peanuts and shellfish.
Two countries were interested in the project, *i.e.*, France and Canada.
Harris enjoys classical music, *that is (to say)* Brahms and Chopin.
I am interested in linguistics, *or* the scientific study of language.
ICBMs, *i.e./or/that is/namely* intercontinental ballistic missiles, are very threatening weapons.

- **Types of apposition relationship**

The appositive directly follows the head noun it defines, and they are usually separated by commas, dashes, or parentheses if the appositive provides non-essential information. There are two types of apposition: **restrictive apposition** and **non-restrictive apposition**.

My old friend *Richard* gave me some good advice. (restrictive)
Richard, *my old friend*, gave me some good advice. (non-restrictive)
An American linguist Noam Chomsky is famous for his theory of generative grammar.
Noam Chomsky, *an American linguist and political activist*, is famous for his theory of generative grammar.
My friend Noam Chomsky is famous for generative grammar.
Noam Chomsky, *my supervisor*, is famous for generative grammar.
John Bunyan, *an English writer*, wrote *The Pilgrim's Progress*.

As shown in the above examples, **restrictive apposition** provides essential information that defines the head (no commas). There are no commas because the specification of the name *Richard* in the first example above is necessary to understand the sentence. **Non-restrictive apposition** adds extra, non-essential information about the head (commas, dashes, or parentheses are used). The commas indicate that *my old friend* in the second example above is additional information and not necessary for the core meaning of the sentence.

3.1.7 Noun phrase coordination: structure and ambiguity

Two or more noun phrases can be coordinated with *and* or *or*, creating various structures of noun phrases as follows:

[[The old man] *and* [his curious dog]] (NP and NP)
[[sports cars] *and* [pickup trucks]] (NP and NP)
[[A few interesting books] *or* [several magazines]] (NP and NP)
[[Red cars], [blue trucks], *and* [green motorcycles]] (NP, NP, and NP)
[[Spicy *and* aromatic] curry] (coordinated parts of an NP: curry that is both spicy and aromatic)
[a mix of [nuts *and* dried fruit]] (coordinated parts of an NP: a mix that consists of both nuts and dried fruit)

mechanical *and* electrical systems (omission of a repeated noun: mechanical systems and electrical systems)
urban *and* rural areas (urban areas and rural areas)
public *or* private institutions (public institutions or private institutions)
positive *and* negative effects (positive effects and negative effects)
his book and magazine (his book and his magazine)

The ambiguity in the following examples arises because the adjective or determiner can apply to both coordinated elements or only to one, depending on the intended meaning.

tall buildings and trees
Reading 1: tall buildings and tall trees
Reading 2: trees and tall buildings

old books and magazines
Reading 1: old books and old magazines
Reading 2: magazines and old books

her pens and other writing supplies
Reading 1 Her pens and her other writing supplies
Reading 2 other writing supplies and her pens

3.1.8 Complex noun phrases

Noun phrases can be very complex through the use of embedded clauses and coordinated noun phrases, as illustrated below:

- [The company *that develops cutting-edge software for data analytics and machine learning*]$_S$ introduced a new platform to the market, which includes [the tools *that provide real-time data analysis and predictive modeling for business intelligence*]$_{DO}$.
- [The team of scientists *who study marine ecosystems and oceanic*

conservation efforts]$_S$ published [their latest research findings *which reveal the changes in coral reef health and the impact of climate change on marine biodiversity*]$_{DO}$.

3.1.9 Function of noun phrases

Various functions of noun phrases are listed as follows:

1. Subject
The old man in the blue hat walked along the street.

2. Subject complement
The problem is *the lack of resources.*

3. Indirect object
He sent *his parents* a postcard.

4. Direct object
She read *the book about ancient civilizations.*

5. Object complement
They elected him *president of the company.*

6. Prepositional complement
She is interested in *marine biology.*

7. Appositive
My brother, *a skilled carpenter*, built the bookshelf.

8. Pre-modifier
I like *science* fiction.
The *coffee* table is very expensive.
Coffee consumption is increasing every year.
The issue will be addressed at the next *Board of Directors* meeting.
The decision was made by the *Human Resources* department.
He attended the *Public Relations* workshop last week.

9. Adverbial

We finished the assignment *last week*.

If you want to get better results, you should handle the task *this way*.

You won't be able to solve it if you keep thinking about it *that way*.

10. Dependent/Independent genitive

According to *the company*'s policy, employees must submit their vacation requests at least two weeks in advance.

This company's policy is different from *the company*'s that we discussed in the previous meeting.

3.2 Verb phrases (VP)

Verb phrases express various grammatical properties of the verb, such as tense, aspect, mood, or voice.

3.2.1 Structure of the verb phrase

A verb phrase typically includes the optional auxiliaries and a main verb (head), as shown in the following:

Structure of verb phrases

(auxiliary 1) modal+**base**	(auxiliary 2) Perfect (have+**pp**)	(auxiliary 3) Progressive (be+-**ing**)	(auxiliary 4) Passive (be+**pp**)	main verb
				succeeded
can				succeed
	have			gone
		was		painting
			was	painted
could	have	been		painting
may	have	been	being	implemented

Based on various combinations of optional auxiliaries and the main verb, we can have many more different patterns than these examples in the table.

3.2.2 Main verbs

The main verb in a sentence conveys the central action, state, or occurrence. It is the core element of the verb phrase and determines the overall meaning of the sentence. As mentioned earlier, regular verbs have four forms, while irregular verbs have five, considering that some irregular verbs have different past and past participle forms.

1. The base form (jump, talk, discuss; sing, write)
2. *-s* form (jumps, talks, discusses; sings, writes)
3. *-ing* form (jumping, talking, discussing; singing, writing)
4. *-ed/-en* form (jumped, talked, discussed; sang/sung, wrote/written)

Anomalous verbs do not conform to the typical patterns of conjugation, unlike regular verbs, which follow a predictable pattern. For example, The verb *be* has eight forms (be; is, am, are; being; was, were; been), especially based on tense, person, and number, and *go* has five forms, including a very peculiar form (go; goes; going; went; gone).

1. The base form: be
2. *-s* form: is, am, are
3. *-ing* form: being
4. *-ed/-en* form: was, were; been

3.2.3 Finite and non-finite verb phrases

Finite and non-finite verb phrases differ in their grammatical functions and in how they relate to the subject of the sentence. A **finite verb phrase** contains one finite verb, which can be marked for person, number, and tense. In a finite verb phrase, the first or only verb is finite, while any other verbs are non-finite, as shown in the following:

She *eats* breakfast every morning. (Present tense, third person singular)
They *were* watching a movie. (Past tense, third person plural)
I *am* going to the store. (Present tense, first person singular)

Finite verbs are necessary for forming a complete sentence or independent clause.

Non-finite verb forms that are not marked for tense, person, or number are as follows:

1. Infinitives: The base form of the verb, often preceded by *to*.
She may *play* the violin at night.
(cf. She *plays* the violin at night.)
She wants *to buy* a new violin.
Steve is afraid *to speak* in public.
I did *clean* the room.

2. *-ing* forms
I enjoy *watching* movies on weekends.
I admit *having* joined the event.
She is *playing* the cello beautifully.
Having finished her homework, Sarah went out to meet her friends.

3. *-ed* Participles:
The old house was *built* ten years ago.

Her plans having been *approved*, she began the project immediately.
The novel, *written* by an unknown author, became a bestseller.

3.2.4 Tense

Tense refers to the time at which an action, state, or event/situation occurs, relative to the moment of speaking. Strictly speaking, English is said to have two primary tenses based on how finite verb forms change: present and past.

1. Present tense

- **Habitual actions or routines**: The present tense is used to describe actions that occur regularly or as part of a routine.

  She writes every day.
  He works in the company.

- **Ongoing states (permanent or long-term)**: The present tense is also used for states that are ongoing and typically permanent or long-term.

  Jennifer lives in Boston.

- **Present facts or relationships**: The present tense is often used to express facts or relationships that are currently true.

  They are my neighbors.

- **General truths**: The present tense is used to express universal truths or scientific facts.

  The sun rises in the east.
  Water boils at 100°C.

- **Immediacy and vividness**: The present tense can also convey a sense of immediacy or vividness, particularly in narrative contexts or sports commentary, making the action feel as if it is happening right now, even if it is not. This use of the present tense brings energy and urgency to the description.

Sports Commentary:
Son passes the ball quickly.
The athlete runs the final lap with incredible speed.

- **Historical present**: The present tense is sometimes used to describe events from the past as if they are happening in the present, a style known as the historical present. This use of the present tense makes past events feel more immediate and vivid.

Caesar crosses the Rubicon.
In 1492, Columbus sails across the ocean.

2. Past tense:

The past tense describes actions or states that were completed in the past, i.e., at some point before the present.

She wrote a letter yesterday. (action in the past)
He was a teacher at that time. (state or role/job in the past.)

3. Future time

The modal verb *will* (also *shall* in British English) is usually used to describe situations in the future. In addition, there are several other ways to express future time.

- **Will**: spontaneous predictions, promises, or decisions

It will rain tomorrow. (prediction)
I will help you with your homework. (promise or offering)
I'll take the job. (decision)

- **be going to**: plans or intentions, and reliable predictions

I'm going to visit my friend next week. (premeditative activity)
Look at those dark clouds. It's going to rain soon. (prediction)
She'*s going to* stay at home during the weekend. (premeditative)

- **Present progressive**: arranged events or scheduled plans

I'm moving to London in December. (arranged or scheduled plan)
We're having a discussion about climate justice next week. (arranged)
I'm going to the BTS concert tomorrow. (arranged event)

- **Present tense**: timetables, programs, or fixed schedules

The train leaves at 6 p.m. tomorrow. (timetable)
The concert starts at 8 o'clock next Friday. (program)
The conference begins at 9 a.m. on Monday. (fixed schedule)

The following hierarchy indicates the increasing certainty or probability of the future situation as follows:

will < be going to < present progressive < present tense

3.2.5 Aspect

Aspect refers to how an action or event expressed by a verb is viewed or understood in relation to time. It provides more detail about the nature of the situation, such as whether it is ongoing or completed over a period. Aspect does not place a situation in a specific time frame and instead, it explains how the situation unfolds over time. There are two main aspects: **progressive** and

perfect. The formats of these two aspects are presented in the table below.

Perfect aspect and progressive aspect

	perfect	progressive
present	have/has studied	is/am/are studying
past	had studied	was/were studying

1. Progressive aspect

The progressive aspect (also known as the continuous aspect) describes situations or events that are ongoing or in progress at a specific time. It focuses on the duration or the process of the action. The progrssive aspect is represented by the auxiliary verb *be* plus *-ing* participle (present participle) of a main verb, as shown in the following:

They *are watching* a movie. (present progressive: ongoing in the present, not completed)
Joan *was reading* a book when I called her. (past progressive: ongoing at a specific time in the past, not completed)

2. Perfect aspect

The perfect aspect describes situations or events that have occurred over an indefinite period of time and have relevance to the present or to another specific time (such as a specific point in the past or future). The perfect aspect is formed with the auxiliary verb *have* plus *-ed* participle (past participle) of a main verb as shown in the following examples:

Samuel *has finished* his homework. (present perfect: completed at some

unspecified time before now, and it is relevant to the present)
He *had finished* his research before the conference started. (past perfect: completed before another action in the past)
He *had* already *left* when she arrived (completed before another action in the past)

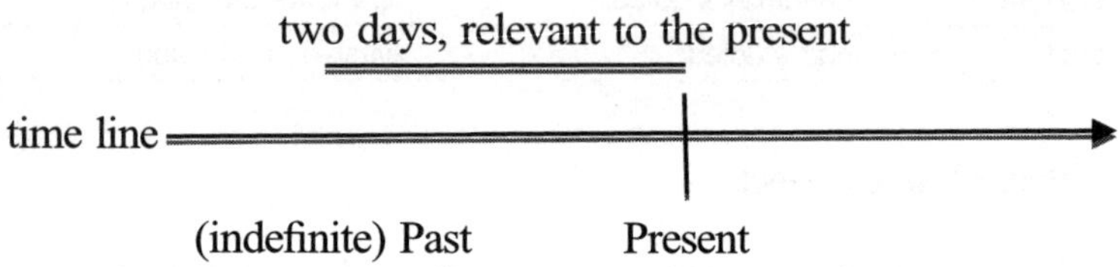

I *have worked* for two days. (indefinite past time, an action that started in the past and has relevance to the present; while the starting time (two days ago) is specified, the present perfect aspect does not focus on a definite point in the past. It rather emphasizes the duration or relevance to the present.)

I *worked* yesterday (definite past time, not relevant to the present)

3.2.6 Voice

In English grammar, **voice** refers to the relationship between the action expressed by a verb and the participants in situations, such as the arguments (subject, object, etc.). It indicates whether the subject performs the action or receives it. There are primarily two voices: **active** and **passive**.

1. Active voice

In the active voice, the subject of the sentence performs the action expressed by the verb. The focus is on the agent (i.e., doer) of the action. The active has the structure of Subject + Verb + Object.

[The cat]$_S$ [chased]$_V$ [the mouse]$_{DO}$.

The active voice is commonly used to emphasize who is performing the action. It provides a direct and clear expression of actions and is often preferred for its straightforwardness and clarity.

2. Passive voice

In the passive voice, the subject of the sentence is affected by the action that the verb expresses. The focus shifts from the agent of the action to the recipient of the action. The passive structure is Subject + *be* verb form (based on tense, person, number) + -*ed* participle + (by + Agent)

[The mouse]$_S$ [was chased]$_V$ ([by the cat]).

The mouse is affected by or receives the action of being chased, and *the cat*, the original agent, is mentioned at the end (optional). The passive voice is used to emphasize the action itself or the recipient of the action rather than the doer.

It is often used in contexts where the agent is unknown, unimportant, less relevant to the context, or unnecessary to mention. These are referred to as **agentless passives,** as shown in the following:

The documents *were stolen* last night.
The decision *has been made.*
The car *was repaired* yesterday.

The window *was broken* during the storm.
The report *was completed* ahead of schedule.

In all these examples, the emphasis is placed on the action itself rather than who performed it. The passive voice is more commonly used used in formal or scientific writing where the focus is on processes, results, or the affected elements. The passive voice can be formed by the following rule.[40]

S V DO
1 2 3 → 3 2 (appropriate form of *be*) V-*ed* (by 1)
Active voice → Passive voice

The chef prepared the meal. → The meal was prepared by the chef.
(focuses on the agent) (focuses on the affected role)

Some more examples are below.

Active	vs	**Passive**
loves		is loved
sold		was/were sold
is fighting		is being fought
has reconstructed		has been reconstructed
will proclaim		will be proclaimed
should be purifying		should be being purified

In the case of sentences with ditransitive verbs, two passives are possible, as follows:

She gave him a gift. → He was given a gift (by her).

40 For detailed discussion on the rule and examples, refer to Akmajian and Henry 1975.

She gave a gift to him. → A gift was given (to)[41] him (by her).

Some sentences can use prepositions other than the typical agentive *by*, such as *at*, *in*, *with*, or *about*, which weaken the agent's role, as shown in the examples below:

Allan *was pleased* with the results.
Many people *were interested* in the Constitution.
James *was surprised* at the news.
Jade *was shocked* at the news.
Stephanie *was concerned* about the project.

As the above examples show, the agent's role becomes less prominent or even de-emphasized; rather, the prepositional complements indicate the reasons for the situations expressed by the verbs. In addition, the *-ed* participle forms can be modified by *very*, illustrating that the participles are used as adjectives.

There are some criteria for distinguishing passive participles (*-ed* participles) from adjective participles.

- Adjective participles can be modified by the intensifier *very*.

  Allan *was very pleased* with the results.

- Adjective participles can often occur after linking verbs other than *be*, such as *become*.

  Many people *became interested* in the Constitution.

- Adjective participles can be coordinated with another adjective.

41 The preposition *to* is occasionally omitted, more commonly in British English (Azar 2002, Swan 2005, among others).

Stephanie *was both happy and concerned* about the project.

- Adjective participles are usually emotional, describing a state or condition of the subject resulting from an action, rather than the action itself.
- Participles with the prefix *-un* are adjective participles.

William was entirely *uninterested* in math.
Because the sky was clear in the morning, the storm was *unexpected.*
Plenty of seats were *unsold* when I phoned the ticket office.

3.2.7 Mood

Mood in grammar refers to the grammatical category that expresses the speaker's attitude toward the situation described and is expressed through different forms of a verb. In other words, mood shows the mode of the situation. There are three primary moods in English: indicative, subjunctive, and imperative.

1. Indicative mood

The **indicative mood** is used to make factual statements, ask questions, or express opinions and exclamations. It is the most commonly used mood in English. The verb forms in the indicative mood vary according to person, number, tense, and aspect.

She *is reading* a book. (a statement of fact)
Are they *coming* to the party? (a question seeking information)
He *does not like* broccoli. (a statement expressing a negative fact)
What a wonderful day it *is*! (exclamations)

2. Imperative mood

The **imperative mood** is used to give commands, make requests, or provide instructions. It directly addresses someone and tells them what to do.

Close the window. (a direct command)
Please *pass* me the salt. (a polite request)
Turn left at the intersection. (an instruction)

As shown in the above examples, the base form of the verb is normally used without a subject. The subject is implied to be *you*. To make a command negative, *do not* or *don't* is used (*Do not be late* or *Don't forget*).

3. Subjunctive mood

The **subjunctive mood** is used to express situations that are mandatory, hypothetical, contrary to fact, wished for, or desired. It conveys actions or states that are not actual, but imagined, suggested, or necessary. The subjunctive mood often appears in *that*-clauses and is triggered by verbs or expressions that indicate necessity, recommendation, suggestion, or desire, which is known as the **mandative subjunctive**. Verbs in *that*-clauses must be in their base form.

- **Mandative subjunctives** (urgency, necessity, importance, recommendation, suggestion, request)

It is crucial that he (should) *be* here.
It is essential that he (should) *be* on time.
It is important that he (should) *be* here on time.
It is necessary that he (should) *be* here on time.

She made a request that the meeting *be* rescheduled to next week.
John proposed that she *attend* the conference next month.

We recommend that he {accept / not accept / should accept / accepts (BE)} their offer.

The committee proposes that the project {be / not be / should be / *is} adopted.

The use of *should* in those relevant sentences is more common in British English, while the base form of the main verb is more common in American English. In British English, verbs (except for *be*) can take the indicative form.[42] The **mandative subjunctive** is often used in *that*-clauses after verbs like *propose*, *suggest*, *move*, *insist*, *demand*, *require*, *request*, and *recommend*.

The mandative subjunctive is used in some fixed expressions as follows:

Long live freedom!
God bless you.
God/Heaven forbid!
He was, *as it were*, the heart of the team
We promised to help the team *come what may*.
Come April/next year, we will move to London.

- ***Were*** **subjunctives** (hypothetical or contrary to fact conditions)

42 For further details, see Huddleston and Pullum 2002.

If he { *were* / was (not formal) } more experienced, he *would* get the job.

If I *were* you, I *would* accept the offer.
(the indicative verb form *was* in informal style)
I *wish* he *were* here.
(wished for or desired situations: things that are imagined)

- **Hypothetical past and past perfective**: use of past indicative forms

If they *invited* John to the international conference, he *would attend.* (hypothetical past)
If they *had invited* him to the international conference, he *would have attended.* (hypothetical past perfective)
If we *had taken* the earlier flight, we *wouldn't have missed* the meeting.
If I *had studied* harder, I *would have passed* the exam.
I *wish* I *had studied* harder for the exam.
I *wish* he *had told* me about the problem earlier.

3.2.8 Multi-word verbs

Multi-word verbs consist of a main verb combined with one or more particles (prepositions or adverbs). These combinations often have meanings that are different from the individual words. Multi-word verbs can be categorized into different types based on their structure.

Types of multi-word verbs

1. **Phrasal verbs**: A type of multi-word verb consisting of a main verb and a particle (which is typically an adverb). The meaning of the phrasal verb is often idiomatic and not always directly derived from the meanings of the individual words.

Please *turn up* the music.
Please *turn* the music *up*.
Please *turn* it *up*.
*Please *turn up* it.

He decided to *give up* smoking.
He decided to *give* smoking *up*.
He decided to *give* it *up*.
*He decided to *give up* it.

In the sentences above, *turn up* and *give up* are transitive phrasal verbs. The nominal object can be placed before or after the particle, but the pronominal object cannot occur after the particle.

Multi-word verbs like *break down*, *show up*, and *wake up* can function as intransitive or transitive phrasal verbs, as shown in the sentences below.

My car *broke down* on the way home.
They *broke* the door *down*.

She *wakes up* early every morning.
My brother *woke* me *up* early in the morning.

A famous singer *showed up* on stage.
She *showed* him *up* in the classroom.

Intransitive phrasal verbs are used in the sentences below.

Please *come in* and have a seat.
He promised to *come back* after lunch
The concert *went on* until midnight.

2. Prepositional verbs: These verbs consist of a main verb followed by a preposition. The **prepositional complement** (usually a noun or noun phrase) must immediately follow the preposition.

They { *depended on him* / **depended him on* }. for help

She { *believes in God.* / **believes God in.* }.

Look at that beautiful painting!
**Look* that beautiful painting *at*!

There are three types of prepositional verbs:
1. My teacher *asked for* help. (prep. verb+dO)
2. I *congratulated* her *on* her promotion. (prep. verb+dO+PP)
3. They warned travelers about HIV infection risks in Africa. (prep. verb+iO 'recipient'+PP)

3. Phrasal-prepositional verbs

Phrasal-prepositional verbs consist of three components: a main verb, a particle (often an adverb), and a preposition. Together, these verbs convey more complex or idiomatic meanings compared to simple phrasal verbs or prepositional verbs, as follows.

I am *looking forward to* the holiday season.
He can't *put up with* the noise any longer.
I *came up with* a brilliant idea for the project out of the blue.
I really *get along with* my coworkers.

Unlike the above examples, the following phrasal-prepositional Verbs require a direct object and a prepositional complement.

Joan didn't want to go to the party, but Shelly *put* her *up to* it.
Why don't you *talk* him *out of* it?

3.3 Adjective phrases (AP)

3.3.1 The structure of the adjective phrase

An adjective phrase refers to a group of words that work together to modify a noun or pronoun, providing more detail or description about it. Its structure can be described as follows:

[(pre-modifiers)	**adjective**	**(post-modifiers)]$_{AP}$**
(so)	pleased	
(so)	pleased	about/with the news
(very)	pleased	to tell you that …
(very)	pleased	that she has got the job

- **Pre-modifiers**: These are usually adverb phrases (often intensifiers) that modify the adjective (*very*, *so*, *extremely*, etc.).
- **Adjective**: The adjective is the main word in the phrase, which describes the noun or pronoun.
- **Post-modifiers**: These are additional phrases or clauses that provide extra information, such as prepositional phrases or clauses (*about the news*, *to tell you that …*, *that she has got the job*).

Some adjectives must be followed by post-modifiers to provide more detail or complete their meaning. These post-modifiers are usually prepositional phrases, *to*-infinitive clauses, or *that*-clauses. In these cases, the post-modifier functions as a complement, giving further information about the adjective.

Jenny's fond *of her pets*. (=Jenny likes her pets.)
John's style is similar *to Jane's*.
Sarah was loath *to tell her mother what had happened.*
We're willing *to discuss the political issue.*
I was not inclined *to get up early in the morning.* (= I didn't want …)
Joe was conscious *that the situation was getting out of hand.*
(=Joe knew that …)

3.3.2 Functions of the adjective phrase

Adjective phrases can perform various functions within sentences as follows:

1. Pre-modifier in a noun phrase

The *happy* children played in the park.
The *exceptionally talented* musician won the award.

2. Post-modifier in a noun phrase

She wore something *special* for her birthday party.
They looked for those *interested in the project.*

3. Subject complement

The paintings were *very beautiful* and *impressive.*
Their approach is *similar to ours.*

4. Object complement

They found the movie *interesting.*
I consider him *very brilliant.*

5. Adjectives as nouns

The poor need our help.
The young are the future of the country.

Shelters are crucial for *the homeless* during the winter.
The elderly require additional support and healthcare services.
The latest was a surprise to everyone.

When adjectives function as nouns after *the*, they are called **nominal adjectives**, which represent abstract entities or a class or group of people or things described by the adjective. Nominal adjectives are also used in fixed expressions that convey a specific meaning, as shown in the examples below.

I'm leaving *for good.*
Are you coming to the party? Yes, *for sure.*
She is *by far* the best candidate for the job.
It was raining, but *at least* it wasn't snowing.

3.4 Adverb phrases (AdvP)

3.4.1 The structure of the adverb phrase

An adverb phrase refers to a phrase that modifies a verb, adjective, or adverb. Its structure can be described as follows:

[(pre-modifiers)	**adverb**	**(post-modifiers)]$_{AdvP}$**
	amazingly	
very	*amazingly*	
very	*amazingly*	*indeed*

3.4.2 Functions of adverb phrases

Adverb phrases serve several key functions:

1. **modifier** of an adjective or an adverb in phrase structure

   a. modifier of an adjective
   The test results were [*surprisingly* good].
   The movie was [*incredibly* entertaining].

   b. modifier of an adverb
   She answered the question [*quite* confidently].
   The chef prepared the dish [*unusually* quickly].

2. **Adverbial** in sentence structure
   I [*completely*] understand your point of view.
   [*Luckily*], our team managed to finish the project ahead of schedule.

3.5 Prepositional phrases (PP)

3.5.1 The structure of the prepositional phrase

A **prepositional phrase** refers to a phrase that starts with a preposition and includes the complement of the preposition along with any modifiers, which is described as follows:

[(pre-modifier)	**preposition**	**complement]** $_{PP}$
	in	*the classroom*
	on	*the table*
just	*after*	*dinner*

The task was completed *with remarkable speed.*
He will arrive *in the early morning*.
She danced *with great grace and style.*
He visits his grandparents *on a regular basis*.
She sings *with remarkable skill.*

- Prepositional phrases containing an NP as a pre-modifier

The house is located two miles *beyond the city limits.*
The report was submitted several hours *after the meeting.*
The lost keys were found five steps *away from the entrance.*
She arrived ten minutes *before the start of the movie.*
The bird perched a few inches *above the ground.*
The assignment was completed half a day *before the deadline.*

In each of these above examples, the structure is maintained with a pre-modifier (noun phrases), followed by a preposition and its complement.

The boat is anchored directly *under the bridge.*
Her performance was well *beyond the limits of what was expected.*
The hotel is quite *near the station.*
Right *after the concert*, we went to a nearby café.

In these above examples, adverbs like *directly*, *well*, *quite*, and *right* function as pre-modifiers and enhance the meaning of the phrase.

- **complements of prepositional phrases**

The complement of a prepositional phrase is the noun phrase or clause that completes the meaning of the preposition.

1. Noun Phrases
She sat *on the bench.*
They walked *through the park.*
He was looking *for her.*

2. Nominal (relative) clauses

She is interested *in what you told her.*

They argued *over what should be done next.*

I'm not interested in whoever you like.

3. Interrogative clauses

He was concerned about *who would take care of the dog.*

4. Noun clause with *that*

She is fortunate in *that she has a supportive family.*

The book is valuable in *that it provides practical advice.*

5. *-ing* clauses

He is interested in *learning new languages.*

She is known for *baking the best cakes in town.*

He succeeded despite *having many challenges.*

She became famous globally after *winning the Nobel Prize.*

6. Prepositional phrases (Nested Prepositional Phrases)

The cat emerged from *under the desk* when it heard the can opener.

The noise from *across the street* was very loud.

A voice was heard from *behind the curtain.*

She pulled the old files from *under the desk.*

- **Stranded prepositions** occur when a preposition is left at the end of a clause or sentence, rather than being placed before its complement. This construction is very common in informal style and certain types of questions, relative clauses, and passive sentences. Stranded prepositions are often associated with more natural, conversational English, whereas fronting the preposition (placing it before the complement) tends to be more formal.

1. Questions:
What are you talking *about*?

2. Relative clauses:
The book you were looking *for* is on the table.

3. Passive sentences
The problem has been dealt *with* by the team.

- **Pied-piping**[43] is a linguistic term used to describe a phenomenon in which a preposition is moved to the front of a relative clause, question, or other clause, along with its complement or the entire phrase it governs. This construction is often more formal and is contrasted with 'stranding.'

The book *to which* I referred is out of print.
To whom did you give the letter?

3.5.2 Functions of prepositional phrases

1. Post-modifier of a noun
The book *on the table* is for you.

2. Post-modifier of an adjective
She is excited *about the trip*.

3. Adverbial (complement)
She sings *with great passion.*
She lives *in Boston.*

43 This is a concept introduced by Ross in 1967.

Exercises

1. Identify whether each *italicized* noun phrase contains a pre-modifier, a post-modifier, both, or neither.

   (1) *The charming little café on the corner* is my favorite spot.
   (2) We discovered *a path leading to the hidden waterfall* during our hike.
   (3) *The mysterious old book in the attic* held many secrets.
   (4) They found *an apartment overlooking the river that they loved.*
   (5) *The exciting new exhibit at the museum* opens next week.

2. Combine each pair of sentences by using relatives.

   (1) a. The researcher discovered a new treatment for the disease.
       b. The treatment has shown promising results in clinical trials.
   (2) a. The artist created a stunning mural.
       b. The mural depicts scenes from local history.
   (3) a. The conference will feature several keynote speakers.
       b. The speakers are experts in their respective fields.

3. Identify the function of each *italicized* NP in the sentences.

   (1) *The historic building* was renovated last year, and *the new facade* impressed everyone.

(2) *The celebrated artist* painted *a mural* for *the community* center, which became a local landmark.

(3) *The delicious meal at the restaurant* left *a lasting impression* on *the guests*.

4. Identify whether the *italicized* clause is a relative clause or an appositive clause.

(1) The scientist discovered a method *that significantly reduces waste in manufacturing.*

(2) We celebrated the decision *that new policy would be implemented next month.*

(3) He expressed his belief *that climate change poses a serious threat to future generations.*

5. Identify whether the *italicized* words are passive participles or adjectives.

(1) The project has been *completed* ahead of schedule.

(2) She felt *relieved* after hearing the good news.

(3) The cookies were *baked* to perfection and smelled delicious.

(4) He was *thrilled* to receive the award for his hard work.

(5) They felt *excited* about the upcoming trip to Hawaii.

6. Identify whether the *italicized* verb is indicative, imperative, mandative, or *were* subjunctive.

(1) They *finished* the project on time.

(2) The manager demanded that he *submit* the report immediately.

(3) She speaks as if she *were* an expert.

(4) It is essential that she *be* on time.

(5) When you arrive, *call* me.

Chapter 4

Sentence Types and Structure

Objectives

- To identify the different types of sentences
- To understand speech acts and their roles in sentence structure
- To understand the functions and structures of clauses
- To understand *there*, cleft, and anticipatory *it*-constructions

Key words

declarative, interrogative, imperative, exclamatory sentences, speech acts (illocution), verbless clauses, existential *there*-constructions, cleft sentences, anticipatory *it*-constructions

Understanding sentences and clauses is fundamental to grasping grammar. Below is a comprehensive summary of sentences and clauses, including their types and functions.

4.1 Sentences

As mentioned in Chapter 1, a sentence is traditionally considered the largest grammatical unit and typically consists of a subject and a predicate, though it can be difficult to define due to various factors. It expresses a complete thought. This notional definition is complemented by a formal definition, which includes punctuation: a sentence begins with a capital letter and ends with a period, question mark, or exclamation mark in writing.

- **Sentences vs. irregular sentences**

  A (regular) sentence, as a grammatical unit, follows a standard structure, such as the seven sentence patterns, typically consisting of a subject and a predicate, and conveys a complete thought. In contrast, irregular sentences deviate from these structures, often omitting elements like subjects, verbs, auxiliaries, or articles. These deviations are common in casual speech or specific contexts, such as sentence fragments. Examples include responses like *Your approval* (an answer to "What do you want from me?"), and news headlines like *Fire destroys downtown building*, *Lost dog found near park*, and *Police investigating downtown shooting*. Fragments usually leave out parts of the sentence that can easily be inferred from context and reconstructed into regular sentences.

- **Non-Sentences** are expressions that do not follow the traditional grammatical structures of sentences and cannot be analyzed as complete sentences. While they lack the necessary components of a standard sentence (such as a subject and a verb), some can still convey complete thoughts, while others do not stand alone as complete thoughts. Non-sentences are commonly used in casual speech, greetings (*Good morning*), advertisements (*Black Friday Sales*), headlines (*War between Ukraine and Russia*), and signs (*No Parking*), where brevity is prioritized.

4.2 Types of sentences

4.2.1 Declarative sentences

Declarative sentences express statements and typically have the seven basic sentence structures.

We are going to the beach tomorrow.
Ala Moana Beach was full of families enjoying the sunny afternoon.
Despite the challenges they faced along the way, the expedition team successfully reached the summit of the mountain.

In the third example, *Despite the challenges they faced along the way* is a prepositional phrase functioning as an adverbial. Its position is flexible and it can occur sentence-finally, as in *The expedition team successfully reached the summit of the mountain despite the challenges they faced along the way.*

4.2.2 Interrogative sentences

Interrogative sentences express questions and are classified into several types.

1. ***Yes-no* questions**: *Yes-no* questions have the Operator-Subject-Verb structure formed through Subject-Operator Inversion.

   Are you planning to visit the museum this weekend?
   Have you finished your homework yet?
   Could you finish the project as soon as possible?
   Did you enjoy the movie last night?

2. ***Wh*-questions**: *Wh*-words (or *wh*-phrases) such as *who*, *which*,

what, *why*, or *how* occur before the operator in *wh*-questions, as shown in the following examples:

How do you find the balance between your work and life?
What have you enjoyed most about the local culture and community?
What is the reason behind the sudden shift in the schedule?
Which restaurant do you recommend for dinner tonight?

When *wh*-words function as the subject, *wh*-questions have the subject-verb structure as in *Who can help me with this project?*

3. **Alternative questions**: These are a type of question that presents two or more options for the respondent to choose from, often connected by *or*. The options typically follow a *yes-no* question or *wh*-question structure.

Would you like *something to eat or something to nibble on*?
Should we meet *in the morning or in the afternoon*?
Are you planning to visit *Paris or London* this summer?
Who would you like to invite to the party, *Joan or John*?
Which would you prefer to do today, *go hiking or visit a museum*?

4. **Tag questions**: The questions are a type of question added to the end of a statement to confirm or check information. They usually consist of an operator and a pronoun. If the statement is positive, the tag question is negative. If the statement is negative, the tag question is positive, as in the following examples:

You're coming to the party, *aren't you*?
You don't like coffee, *do you*?
You're ready for the trip, *aren't you*?

She didn't forget the meeting, *did she*?

Rising intonation in a tag question indeed expresses questioning, implying that the speaker is uncertain or seeking clarification, whereas falling intonation expresses certainty or seeks agreement.

Positive (affirmative) sentences can be followed by positive tag questions to express surprise, concern, or doubt, depending on the context.

You're quitting the job in this economy, *are you*? (This expresses surprise or concern.)

Tag questions such as *will you*, *would you*, *can you*, and *could you* can be used in imperative sentences. They are typically used to make polite requests or seek confirmation in daily conversation.

- ***Will you?*** is the most common form used in polite requests.

Don't leave without saying goodbye, *will you?*
Stay for dinner, *won't you?*
Help me with this project, *will you?*

Will you? sounds a little more straightforward and less polite than *would you* or *could you*, even though it is commonly used in daily conversation.

- ***Would you?*** is often used to make requests sound even more polite, courteous, or formal.

Pass me the salt, *would you?*
Please lend me your notebook, *would you?*

- ***Can you?*** can also be used in tag questions to ask if the listener is capable of doing the requested action.

  Close the window, can you?
  Bring me a glass of water, can you?

It emphasizes the listener's ability to do the action.

- ***Could you?*** is similar to *can you?*, but *could you?* is often more polite, less demanding, or formal and suggests a slightly less direct request.

  Hand me that book, could you?
  Move the table here, could you?

  In *let's* imperatives, *shall we?* is typically used as follows:

  Let's have a break, *shall we?*
  Let's go for a walk, *shall we?*

- **Declarative questions**: Declarative questions are formed by turning a declarative statement into a question, usually with rising intonation. However, when written, they typically end with a question mark rather than a period.

  They finished the project?
  You know the answer?
  She's already left for work?

- **Rhetorical questions**: Rhetorical questions highlight the opposite or reverse effect, emphasizing a point without expecting an answer. They are often used to make a point or emphasize something and are commonly found in persuasive writing, speeches, and conversation.

Who *wouldn't* want a vacation? (implying that everyone *would* want a vacation.)
Who *knows*? (implying that *nobody* knows.)
How many times *do* I *have to tell* you? (implying that I *won't* tell you anymore.)
Who *cares* about that? (implying that *nobody* cares about it.)
How could *anyone* believe that? (implying that *no one* would believe it.)
Can you *imagine* living without technology? (implying that living without technology is almost *unimaginable* or very difficult to conceive. You *can't imagine* living without technology.)

4.2.3 Imperative sentences

They begin with the base form of the verb and express commands, instructions, or requests.

(You) *Close* the window before it rains.
Don't forget your umbrella when you leave.
Please *make* sure to double-check your report before submitting it.
Don't be ripped off. (passive imperative in the negative)

Imperatives for the first person and third person can be formed using *let* followed by a subject. When the speaker does not specify or know who will help, *somebody* is often used to convey that help is needed from anyone.

Somebody *help* me. (third person subject)
Guests *enjoy* the refreshments. (third person subject)
Let me introduce myself. (first person subject)
Let us help them with that. (first person subject)
Let's not waste any time. (first person subject; negative)

Don't let's waste any time. (first person subject; negative)
Let him go. (third person subject)
Let nobody interrupt the meeting. (third person subject)

4.2.4 Exclamatory sentences

Exclamatory sentences are statements that express strong emotions, such as surprise, joy, anger, or excitement. They often begin with *How* or *What* and are typically marked by an exclamation mark at the end. These sentences convey a heightened emotional response and are more intense in tone than a typical declarative sentence.

What a beautiful day!
What a fantastic idea!
How fast time flies!
What a surprise! (I didn't expect to see you here!)

4.3 Positive and negative sentences

Positive and negative sentences are basic types of sentences that convey whether something is positive (affirmative) or negative in meaning.

1. **Positive sentences** state or affirm actions, facts, descriptions, or events. They express agreement or confirmation and do not include any negation words (e.g., *not*, *never*, *no*, *nothing*, etc.).

2. **Negative sentences**, in contrast, typically include those negation words, which usually come after the operator, as in the

examples below:

She *is* studying for her exams. (negative: She *is not* studying …)
The sun *rises* in the east. (negative: The sun *does not rise* …)
She *can* play the cello very well. (negative: She *cannot* play …)
We *have* a meeting tomorrow. (negative: We *don't have* …)

I have *never* seen such a beautiful sunset before.
I have *no* idea what happened to my favorite galaxy tablet.
Nothing can stop us when we work together as a team.

4.4 Speech acts (Illocution)

Speech acts refer to actions realized through speaking or writing, where the act of communication itself accomplishes something beyond merely conveying information—such as making an offer, issuing an apology, giving a promise, offering a warning, giving an order, making a request, giving advice, making a suggestion, lodging a complaint, or extending an invitation, as shown in the examples below:

Can you close the window? (making a request)
Please submit the report by Friday. (giving an order)
I'm so sorry for the mistake. (issuing an apology)
If you're feeling cold, I can give you my jacket. (making an offer)
It might help if you review your notes before the exam. (Giving advice)
Is it okay if I leave early today? (Asking for permission)
I suggest you lock the door before you leave; there's been a lot of activity around here lately. (Giving a warning)
Why don't we take a break for 15 minutes before diving back in? (Making a suggestion)

If you keep leaving your bike in the hallway, I'll have to report it to security. (Making a threat)
Would you like to join us for dinner? (Offering Invitation)

These are the actions performed or realized through speaking. They reflect the speaker's intentions and the function of the utterance within a conversation. Speech acts are essential for understanding how language functions in various contexts.

4.5 Clauses

A clause is a group of words that contains a subject and a predicate. One finite clause can be used as a simple sentence as follows:

I seek refuge in no such excuses.
A painter's monument is his work.
(Somerset Maugham, *The Moon and Sixpence*, p. 8-9)

More than one clause can form multiple sentences, which can be classified into three types.

4.5.1 Three types of multiple sentences

1. **Compound sentences** contain two or more coordinated clauses joined by a coordinating conjunction (*and*, *or*, *but*) or a semicolon.

I wanted to go to the beach, *but* it started raining.
The sun was setting, *and* the sky turned a beautiful shade of orange.

2. **Complex sentences** contain one main clause and at least one subordinate clause usually introduced by subordinators (*because*, *although*, *since*, *whether*, *that*, etc.) or relatives (*who*, *which*, *that*, etc..).

I didn't realize *that* the meeting was rescheduled.
Although it was raining, we decided to go for a walk.
When the movie ended, the audience applauded loudly.
I will call you *if* I finish my work early.
He was surprised *that* she knew so much about the topic.
When so much has been written about Charles Strickland, it may seem unnecessary *that* I should write more.
(Somerset Maugham, *The Moon and Sixpence* p. 8)

3. **Compound-complex sentences** contain two or more coordinated clauses and at least one subordinate clause. Examples are presented below:

Although it was raining, we went to the park *and* had a great time despite the weather.
She went to the store *because* she needed groceries, *and* he stayed home.
He spent the last years of his life in Tahiti, *and* there I came across those *who* were familiar with him. (Somerset Maugham, *The Moon and Sixpence*, p. 8)
There, *as* is notorious, he spent the last years of his life; *and* there I came across persons *who* were familiar with him. (Somerset Maugham, *The Moon and Sixpence*, p. 8)

In the following sentence, *but* connects two coordinated clauses (CL1 and CL2), while the second coordinated clause (CL2) contains a subordinate clause (CL3) introduced by *because*, which provides the reason for misplacing the ticket.

[I bought two concert tickets a week ago]$_{CL1}$, *but* [yesterday I couldn't find the tickets [*because* I misplaced them]$_{CL3}$]$_{CL2}$.

4.5.2 Types of subordinate clauses

1. **Nominal clauses** act as noun phrases in a sentence. They generally function as subjects, subject complements, direct objects, or prepositional complements, and they are introduced by words like *that*, *whether*, *who*, *what* as well as *-ing* participles and *to*-infinitives, as shown in the examples below:

The problem is [*that we don't have enough time*]$_{SC}$.
She asked [*whether they were coming*]$_{DO}$.
I don't know [*who is in charge of the project*]$_{DO}$.
[*What he declared*]$_S$ surprised everyone.
Do [*whatever interests you*]$_{DO}$ when it comes to choosing a job.
[*How he managed to finish the project*]$_S$ is still a mystery.
She was worried about [*how they would react*]$_{PM}$.

2. **Adverbial clauses**

An adverbial clause is a subordinate clause that functions as an adverbial within a sentence, providing additional information about time, place, condition, reason, or manner, etc.

I will call you *when I arrive.*
I will call you, *when I arrive*, to confirm the time.
When I was young, I used to play outside a lot.
He was late *because he missed the bus.*
I will go to the park *if it stops raining.*
Although it rained, we went hiking.
Wherever you go, *whatever you do*, I will be right here waiting for you. (Richard Marx - *Right here waiting for you*)

3. Modifier clauses

A modifier clause modifies nouns, pronouns, or adjectives. It is usually a relative clause introduced by relative pronouns like *who*, *whose*, *whom*, *which*, and *that*, an *-ed* clause, an *-ing* clause, and a *to*-infinitive.

The book *that I borrowed yesterday* is very intriguing.
The conference held in the convention center was a great success.
The movie *starring a famous actor* received excellent reviews.
She was happy *to know that her team won the championship.*

4.5.3 To-Infinitive clauses

A *to*-infinitive clause begins with an infinitive (*to* + the base form of a verb), and it can include modifiers or objects.

1. Subject of a sentence
To travel the world is my dream.

2. Subject complement
His goal is *to become a doctor.*

3. Object of a verb
She hopes *to pass the exam.*

4. Adjective modifier
He was loath *to make a speech before the large audience.*

5. Adverbial
He went to the store *to buy groceries.*

6. Appositive clause
My duty *to help others* comes before my own personal needs.

4.6 Non-finite and verbless clauses

Non-finite clauses and **verbless clauses** are usually regarded as subordinate clauses that differ from finite clauses in their structure and function.

4.6.1 Non-finite clauses contain non-finite verbs (infinitives, *-ing* forms, or *-ed* participles). These clauses often function as nominal, adverbial, or modifier clauses within a sentence.

1. Infinitive clauses

To win the championship was his ultimate goal.
She had strategies *to improve the company's finances.*
The school organized a field trip *to teach students about local history.*
He let them *stay at his house.*

2. *-ing* clauses

Eating too much can lead to health problems.
She enjoys *reading novels in her free time.*
What he enjoys most is *traveling to new countries.*
The man *sitting at the corner table* is my uncle.
Walking quickly, she managed to catch the bus.

3. *-ed* clauses

Confused by the instructions, he asked for clarification.
The conference *held in Seoul yesterday* was a great success.

The *-ing* clauses and *-ed* clauses serve as reduced clauses of finite clauses, as shown in the following:

The woman *sitting at the corner table* is my aunt.
(*... who is sitting at the corner table ...*)
Walking quickly, he managed to arrive at the conference on time.
(*As he walked quickly*, ...)
The conference *held in Seoul yesterday* was a great success.
(*... that was held in Seoul yesterday ...*)
Confused by the instructions, they asked for clarification.
(*Because they were confused by the instructions*, ...)

When the subject of the non-finite clause differs from that of the main clause, it is specified as follows:

I looked at the painting, *my eyes filled with awe.*
I jogged along the beach, *the cool breeze refreshing my spirit.*

4.6.2 Verbless clauses

A verbless clause is a subordinate (i.e., dependent) clause that does not contain a verb. It serves as a reduced clause of a finite clause and can function as an adverbial.

Tired from the long journey, Taylor decided to rest at home.
(*Because she was tired from the long journey*, ...)
Take one pill three times a day *when necessary.*
(Take one pill three times a day *when it is necessary.*)

When the subject of the verbless clause differs from that of the main clause, it is specified as follows:
He spoke at the conference, *his voice steady and calm.*

4.7 Existential *there*-constructions

Existential *there*-constructions are a type of sentence construction used to introduce or emphasize the existence or presence of something (usually new information). The construction typically starts with the expletive *there*, followed by a form of the verb *be* and other similar verbs, and then a subject that is often an indefinite noun phrase, as shown in the following:

There are several issues we need to discuss.
There were many people at the concert last night.
There appears to be some confusion about the schedule.
There occurred a shocking event yesterday.
There is someone who wants to speak with you.
There is nothing more we can do at this point.
There are seats available, aren't there?
There's a few issues we need to discuss. (in informal contexts)[44]
There's/There are interesting books on the desk, aren't there?
There's/There is an interesting book on the desk, isn't there?
There are no seats available, *are there*?

As shown in the examples above, the form of the verb *be* (singular vs. plural) is determined by the subject following it, and the contracted form *there's* can be followed by a plural noun phrase in informal style.

44 The same applies to the sentences *Here's some articles about the issue* and *Where's my socks?*

4.8 Cleft and pseudo-cleft sentences

Cleft and pseudo-cleft sentences are both structures used to emphasize a particular part of a sentence by dividing information into distinct parts.

4.8.1 Cleft sentences

Cleft sentences, as emphatic constructions, highlight a specific element of a sentence. They usually involve splitting a sentence into two parts, where one part is emphasized more than the other. The basic structure of a cleft sentence is 'It is/was + the emphasized part + that + the rest part of the sentence,' as shown in the following:

[Harris]$_{S}$ met [Jane]$_{DO}$ [in the park]$_{A}$ [yesterday]$_{A}$. (neutral sentence)

→ *It was* Harris *that/who* met Jane in the park yesterday.
→ *It was* Jane *that/who(m)* Harris met in the park yesterday.
→ *It was* in the park *that* Harris met Jane yesterday.
→ *It was* yesterday *that* Harris met Jane in the park.

In the above cleft sentences, the emphasized parts are the subject, direct object, and adverbials (indicating place and time). Clauses can be emphasized as follows:

It was when she traveled to South Korea *that* she became interested in Korean culture.
It was because he worked so hard *that* he was promoted.

4.8.2 Pseudo-cleft sentences

Pseudo-cleft sentences, like cleft sentences, are used to emphasize a particular part of a sentence. The structure of a pseudo-cleft sentence is 'What + the rest part (except for an emphasized part) + is + an emphasized part,' as shown in the following:

I want a good rest now.
→ *What I want now is* a good rest.
The new software will improve our productivity.
→ *What will improve our productivity is* the new software.
I'm going to visit the museum tomorrow.
→ *What I'm going to do tomorrow is* (to) visit the museum.
I want to finish the project tomorrow.
→ *What I want is* to finish the project tomorrow.

4.9 Anticipatory *it*-constructions

Anticipatory *it*-construction is a grammatical structure in which *it* functions as a placeholder subject or object, anticipating an extraposed clause. This process, known as extraposition, involves placing a complex subject or object (often a nominal clause) at the end of the sentence. It aligns with the end-weight principle, which places longer or heavier elements at the end to enhance readability and clarity. The typical structure of sentences with anticipatory *it* is as follows:

It + linking verb + Complement + *that/wh*-clause/*to* infinitive.

It is obvious that they made the right decision.
It is important to review the article.

It is necessary to follow the guidelines.
It will be so interesting to check how the new policy affects workers.
It remains uncertain whether he will accept the offer.
It is unclear what caused the accident.
He deemed *it* right to tell the truth.

On the other hand, when an *-ing* clause (gerund phrase) is functioning as the subject of the sentence, it is generally not extraposed in the same way, as in the examples below:

Running every morning keeps me fit.
Playing tennis is fun.

Exercises

1. For each given sentence, identify a potential speech act that could be expressed by the utterance.

   (1) I forgot to bring my book.
   (2) It's really cold in here.
   (3) Be careful on that icy sidewalk!
   (4) If I were you, I would take that job offer.
   (5) If only I could travel to Paris this summer.

2. Identify the function (S, V, SC, etc.) of the *italicized* part in the non-finite or verbless clause in each sentence.

   (1) Preparing *the meal* for the party took longer than expected.
   (2) *The weather* being perfect, we decided to have a picnic in the park.
   (3) You can improve your skills by practicing *regularly*.
   (4) They hope to complete the project *ahead of schedule*.
   (5) They are satisfied with living *in Boston*.
   (6) They promised to send *the customers* their orders promptly.

3. Turn the following sentences into sentences with anticipatory *it*.

   (1) Where they will go on vacation is still undecided.
   (2) Whether she can finish the project on time is still uncertain.

(3) That he passed the exam was a pleasant surprise.
(4) To learn a new language can be challenging.

4. Identify the type of each italicized clause (comparative/adverbial/nominal/nominal relative/relative/reduced relative clause)

(1) *Whoever arrives first* gets the best seat.
(2) He didn't believe *what they told him.*
(3) I saw the student *whose essay won the first prize in the competition.*
(4) This is the reason *why I called you.*
(5) The book *borrowed from the library* is due next week.
(6) Students *attending the seminar* must arrive on time.
(7) She stayed inside *because it was raining heavily.*
(8) She is taller *than I expected.*
(9) She runs as fast *as her brother does.*

5. Convert the sentences into cleft sentences in which the *italicized* part is emphasized.

(1) *The teacher* praised the students.
(2) They are planning *a surprise party.*
(3) I saw her at the concert *last night.*
(4) We had dinner *at the new restaurant.*
(5) He traveled to Paris *because he wanted to explore new cultures.*

6. Rewrite the sentence into a pseudo-cleft structure that emphasizes

the italicized part.

(1) I appreciate *the support from my friends* the most.

(2) She craves *a slice of chocolate cake*.

(3) The team needs *a strong leader*.

Chapter 5

Major Grammatical Usages

Objectives

To understand various grammatical usages, including:

- Number agreement in sentences
- Case usage (pronouns, complements)
- Issues with multiple negation
- The usages of adjectives, adverbs, and comparison
- Specific types of adverbial clauses
- Special constructions

Key words

number agreement, proximity agreement, collective nouns; case, subject complement, pronoun case, relative pronouns, subjects in -ing clauses; double/triple negation; adjectives, adverbs, comparison; adverbial clauses, absolute (participial) constructions, dangling modifiers, participle clauses; special constructions

5.1 Number agreement

Number agreement (or concord) refers to the grammatical rule that parts of a sentence, especially the subject and verb, must agree in number (singular or plural) and person (first, second, or third), known as subject-verb agreement.

5.1.1 Subject-verb agreement

The verb in a sentence must agree with the subject in number (singular or plural), and the verb *be* must agree with the subject in both number (singular or plural) and person (first, second, or third person). The head in the noun phrase functioning as the subject determines the subject-verb agreement, as illustrated in the examples below:

The *dog runs* around the park every afternoon.
The *dogs run* around the park every afternoon.

The *dog is* running around the park.
The *dogs are* running around the park.

The *movement* of the dancers *is* mesmerizing the audience.
The *movements* of the dancers *are* mesmerizing the audience.

5.1.2 Compound/Coordinated subjects

When a subject consists of two or more nouns (or noun phrases) connected by *and*, it is typically treated as plural, and the verb must be plural.

Tom *and* Jerry *are* friends.
My dog *and* your cat *are* outside.

If compound or coordinated subjects are treated as a single, combined item, they take singular verbs.

Bread and butter is often the first meal served with milk at breakfast.
(cf. *Bread and butter are* essential for making a quick sandwich.)
Slow and steady wins the race.

In the above sentences, the first *bread and butter* is treated as a single unit (a basic meal), whereas the second *bread and butter* is treated as separate items (i.e., distinct ingredients). *Slow and steady* is treated as a single idea or concept.

5.1.3 Proximity agreement

If the subject nouns are connected by *Either ... or*, *Neither … nor*, *Not only … but also*, *Not … but*, the verb agrees in number with the noun closest to it, which is known as the principle of proximity agreement.

Either the teacher *or the students are* responsible for this project.
Either the students *or the teacher is* responsible for this project.
Neither the manager *nor the employees are* attending the meeting.
Neither the employees *nor the manager is* attending the meeting.
Not only the boss *but also the employees are* working late tonight.
Not only the employees *but also the boss is* working late tonight.
Not the books *but the notebook is* on the table.
Not the notebook *but the books are* on the table.

5.1.4 Prepositional phrases

The subject noun phrase before *as well as*, (*along*) *with*, and *but*—which function as (complex) prepositions—determines the number of the verb.

The boss, as well as the employees, *is* working late tonight.
Lisa, along with her friends, *was* invited to the wedding next month.
Nobody but two members *has* attended the meeting. (but = except for)

5.1.5 Indefinite pronouns

Indefinite pronouns, such as *everyone*, *no one*, *none*, *nobody*, *someone*, etc., are treated as singular.

Everybody has his or her own right to expression.
Someone follows them secretly.
Has anybody called while I was out?
If *anything goes* wrong, let me know immediately.
No one (*of us/his friends) *is* going to attend the meeting. (=Nobody)
None of the information is correct.
None of the students has completed the assignment yet.
(…have… in informal contexts)
None of the paintings in the gallery *was* damaged during the war.
(…were… in informal contexts)
Neither of his parents is going to attend the meeting.
(…are… in informal contexts)
Neither of the solutions is appropriate. (…are… in informal contexts)
Neither solution is appropriate.

5.1.6 Each/Every-phrases

When the subject includes *each* or *every*, it is treated as singular, as shown in the following sequences:

1. Each/Every + sg. noun + sg. verb

Each or *every* is followed by a singular noun, which requires a singular verb.

Each student is required to complete the assignment.
Every book on the shelf *has* been read.

2. Each/Every+sg. noun+and (each/every)+sg. noun+sg. verb

When *each* or *every* is used with two singular nouns connected by *and*, the structure still requires a singular verb, because both nouns are considered individually.

Each teacher and (each) student is responsible for their actions.
Every cat and (every) dog is well-fed at the shelter.

Both of these patterns maintain subject-verb agreement in singular form.

5.1.7 Plural forms as a unit

When plural forms (e.g., *weeks*, *years*, or *dollars*) function as a single concept or unit in terms of time, distance, or amount, they are treated as singular.

Two weeks is enough for you to finish the project. (a single unit)
Three miles is too far to walk. (a single unit)
Ten dollars is all I have in my wallet. (a single unit)
Twenty dollars is enough.(total sum as a single entity)
(cf. *Twenty dollars are* missing: individual dollars or separate units)
Ten years is a long time for them to wait.
(cf. *Ten years have* passed since I saw her last: separate units)

5.1.8 Noun phrase-pronoun agreement

Pronouns must agree in number and gender with the nouns they refer to.

The boy found *his* lost dog in the park.
The boys found *their* lost dogs in the park.

When noun phrases treated as singular include indefinite pronouns or are introduced by indefinite determiners such as *every*, *each*, and *any*, the pronouns *his* and *him* have traditionally been used. To avoid sex bias, it is now more common to use *his or her* and *him or her*. In informal contexts, *their* and *them* are increasingly used as gender-neutral alternatives.

Everyone has *his/his or her/their* freedom of speech and the press.
Each student is responsible for *his/his or her/their* actions.
Does *any student* want to present *his/his or her/their* homework?

5.1.9 Relative clauses

1. Subjective relatives have the same number as their antecedents, as in the examples below:

The students who *are* participating in the project are very dedicated.
The manager who *handles* the finances will be away this week.
The dog that *barks* at night keeps me awake.
The car which *is* parked outside belongs to my neighbor.
The songs that *were* performed at the concert were amazing.
He/One who *helps* himself will find success in the long run.
Those who *help* themselves will find success in the long run.

2. The number agreement of *what* and *whoever* in relative clauses depends on the context, as illustrated in the examples below:

What *drives* him to succeed *is* his passion for the work.
What *matters* most to me *is* the happiness of my family.
What she said in the meeting *was* exactly what I thought.
What she said *was* important.

Give these shoes to *whoever needs* them.

Whoever is in charge of the meeting should be prepared to answer questions.

Whoever finishes their work early can leave for the day.

Whoever arrives first *gets* to choose the movie for tonight.

Whoever makes the most progress will receive a reward.

I will speak to *whoever is* responsible for the project mistake.

Please give the documents to *whoever* you think *needs* them.

Whoever double-parked *has* to move their car immediately.

Whoever double-parks during the meeting *causes* lots of inconvenience.

She will consult *who(m)ever* she deems necessary for the project.

5.1.10 Collective nouns

Collective nouns (e.g., *committee, family, jury, public, team, audience, police, cattle, vermin*) can be singular or plural depending on whether they are viewed as single entities or as individual members.

The team *is* winning. (a single entity)

The team *are* arguing among themselves. (individual members)

The committee *has* reached its decision. (a single entity)

The committee *consists* of nine members. (a single entity)

The committee has/have regular meetings.

The committee was/were pleased with the outcome of the vote.

The committee was/were divided on the issue of funding.

The committee was/were divided in its/their opinion with regard to this issue.

And, in the off-season, <u>the team has decided</u> to audition five flawed quarterbacks for next year's starting role. (*The New Yorker*, May 13, 2013)

The *committee has* argued that claims of executive privilege are not valid for Bannon. (*Washington Post*, July 8, 2022)

… the committee have argued Bannon was never shielded by the former president's claims, as… (*CBS News*, July 11, 2022)

News of the letter, which was addressed to Bannon's attorney, comes as the committee is scheduled to meet Tuesday and vote on whether the Trump ally should be referred to the Justice Department for criminal contempt charges after refusing to comply with the panel's subpoena deadline last week. (*CNN*, October 18, 2021)

… the committee has conducted more than 1,000 interviews …

The committee is reportedly planning to play snippets of testimony … (*The Economist*, June 7, 2022)

In British English, collective nouns often take plural verbs when the noun is regarded as individuals, while in American English, collective nouns tend to take singular verbs even when referring to individuals.

The nouns *police*, *vermin*, and *cattle* are always followed by plural verbs.

The police *were* called to the scene of the accident.

The police *were* conducting interviews with witnesses

The audience *was* captivated by the performance.

Vermin *are* various small, harmful animals or insects that damage crops, spread disease, or cause general nuisance.

Vermin *have* infested the old barn, chewing through the stored grain.

The vermin in the warehouse *were* causing significant damage to the stored food.

The rancher is not going anywhere until the cattle *move* into the fence.

The cattle mow down the fields and then the chickens spread out the manure and aerate the soil … (oregonlive.com (Feb. 13, 2024), "Oregon wine country B&B focuses on connection to the ground")

5.1.11 Other related topics

- The fields of study such as *linguistics*, *physics*, *mathematics*, and *economics*, which end in *-ics*, are treated as singular as follows:

Linguistics *is* the scientific study of language.
Physics *is* my favorite subject.
Statistics *is* the science of collecting, analyzing, and interpreting data.
Statistics *reveal* a significant increase in online shopping over the past decade. (statistical data)

- The names of nations, diseases, games, books, etc., and citations are also treated as singular, as shown in some examples below:

The United States *plays* a significant role in global economic affairs.
The Philippines *is* known for its beautiful beaches.
Measles *is* a highly contagious viral disease.
Mumps *is* an infectious disease.
Billiards *is* one of my favorite games.
Darts *is* one of your favorite games.
The Old Man and the Sea was written by Ernest Hemingway.
Sonyeoni onda (*Human Acts*) *was* written by Han Kang in 2014.
Gisaengchung (Parasite) is a Korean film directed by Bong Joon-ho.
Oxen is a native English plural, whereas *criteria is* the plural form derived from Latin.

- *Many* takes plural nouns and plural verbs, but *many* can also be used with the indefinite article *a* and a single noun, as in *many a student.*

Many students *are* attending the meeting.

Many a student *is* attending the meeting. (more formal and poetic)

- *The number of* … and *a number of* … are followed by plural nouns, but take different verbs in terms of number.

The number of the students who attended the conference *was* ten.
A number of students *were* attending the conference.

- Nouns like *glasses*, *spectacles*, *belongings*, *clothes*, *trousers*, *pants*, *socks*, *scissors*, and others are plural in form, but they often refer to single items (like *a pair of glasses*) or groups of items (like *clothes*). Nevertheless, these nouns are treated as plural, meaning they are followed by plural verbs.

Your glasses *are* very light.
My trousers *have* a coffee stain.

- The phrase *a pair of*, on the other hand, can be used before certain nouns (e.g., *glasses*, *spectacles*, *scissors*, etc.), and when it is used, the subject is considered singular, so it is followed by a singular verb, as shown in the examples below:

A new pair of shoes *is* needed. My old one is threadbare.
A pair of scissors *has* been misplaced in the kitchen.

5.2 Case

As mentioned in Chapter 2, case marks the grammatical function or role of a noun phrase and also indicates grammatical relations between noun phrases in a sentence.

5.2.1 Subject complement

A noun phrase functioning as a subject takes the subjective case form, and one functioning as an object takes the objective case form. A noun phrase used as a subject complement generally takes the subjective case form in formal contexts, while it may take the objective case form in informal contexts, as shown in the examples below:

It was *I* who made the decision. (subjective case: formal context)
It was *me* who made the decision. (objective case: informal context)
It is *he* who should take responsibility for the decision.
It is *him* who should take responsibility for the decision.
Who's there? -- It's *me*.
Who declared the martial law? -- That's *him*.

5.2.2 Pronoun case forms after *as* and *than*

The case of the pronoun after *as* and *than* depends on its function in the comparative construction, as shown in the following examples:

She is as tall as *I (am)/me*. (… as tall as I (am tall); me → informal style)
They like her more than *me*. (They like her more than (they like) me.)
They like her more than *I* (do). (They like her more than I (like her).)

They enjoy fishing more than *I* (do). (… than I (enjoy fishing).)

5.2.3 *but* as a preposition

When *but* is used as a preposition, it takes the objective case form as a prepositional complement.

Everyone but *me* passed the test.
She spoke to everyone but *him* during the meeting.
All but *us* have finished their assignments.

5.2.4 Relative pronouns: *who(m), who(m)ever*

The relative pronouns *who* and *whom* are the subjective and objective case forms and function as a subject and an object, respectively. In informal contexts, *who* is usually used instead of *whom*, as shown in the following examples:

The man *whom/who* you spoke to is my uncle.
The man *to whom/*to who* you spoke is my uncle.[45]
She is the person *whom/who* I trust the most.
Please give the books to students *who* you think need them.
She will consult experts *whom/who* she deems necessary for the project.

The relative pronouns *whoever* and *whomever* function as a subject and an object in relative clauses, respectively:

45 The same applies to questions with *who/whom*: *Whom are you waiting for?* and *For whom are you waiting?* are used in formal contexts, while *Who are you waiting for?* is used in informal contexts. *For who are you waiting?* is not grammatical because the complement of the preposition must be in the objective case form.

Please give the books to *whoever* you think needs them.
She will consult *whomever/whoever* she deems necessary for the project.

In the first sentence, *whoever* functions as the subject of *needs*, while in the second sentence, *whomever* functions as the object of *deems*, in which *whoever* can be used in informal contexts.

5.2.5 Case of a nominal subject in *-ing* clauses

-ing clauses (often called gerund phrases) can have a noun phrase as their subject. The case form of this subject is typically in the genitive (possessive) form, but it can also appear in the common case of a noun or the objective case of a pronoun in more informal contexts.

1. Genitive (possessive) form of the subject

In formal contexts, when a noun or noun phrase is the subject of an *-ing* clause, it typically takes the genitive (possessive) form.

I appreciate *John's* helping me.
She resented *Steve's* making all the decisions.
Do you mind *my* smoking?
I remember *his* helping me with the project last year.
I am grateful for *their* helping me with the presentation.
He was criticized for *his not* following the rules.
I regret *Sarah's* leaving the team.
They appreciated *Mike's* helping with the event.
I don't mind *Tom's* asking for help.
We admired *Emily's* solving the problem so quickly.

2. Objective form of the subject

In informal contexts, it is common for speakers to use the objective form of a pronoun or the non-genitive form (common case) of a noun as the subject of the gerund phrase.

I appreciate *John* helping me.
She resented *Steve* making all the decisions.
Do you mind *me* smoking?
I remember *them* helping me with the project last year.
I am grateful for *them* helping me with the presentation.
I regret *Sarah* leaving the team.
They appreciated *Michael* helping with the event.
I don't mind *Tom* asking for help.
We admired *Emily* solving the problem so quickly.

The non-genitive case (common case) is usually used for long noun phrases and non-personal nouns.

I appreciated *the car* being parked in front of the house, as it made it easier to unload the groceries.
The children enjoyed *the playground* being cleaned every morning.
I remember *the books* being left on the shelf all day.
She didn't mind *the computer* being turned off so frequently.
They were surprised by *the tree* being cut down without any warning.

5.3 Multiple negation

5.3.1 Avoidance of double negation

Double negation, which involves using two negatives to convey a single negative meaning, is generally avoided in standard English. While double negatives can sometimes result in a positive meaning in certain dialects, such as African American Vernacular English, they are typically deemed incorrect in standard usage.

I *don't* have *no* money.(→ I don't have *any* money.)
He *can't* find *nothing* in his bag. (→ He can't find *anything* in his bag.)
We *didn't* do *nothing* wrong. (→ We didn't do *anything* wrong.)
He *won't never* listen to me. (→ He won't *ever* listen to me.)
I'*m not* going *nowhere* today. (→ I'm not going *anywhere* today.)

In the following examples, using double negatives with adverbs like *rarely*, *hardly*, *never*, or *seldom* is also considered incorrect in standard English because it causes unnecessary complexity and can cause confusion. Standard English generally requires only one negative expression to convey the intended meaning clearly.

I *can't barely* hear you.
(→I can barely hear you.)
He *doesn't seldom* make mistakes.
(→ He seldom makes mistakes.)

These examples demonstrate why double negation is deemed incorrect in standard English, as it muddles the intended meaning. In standard usage, a single negation is enough to express the point clearly.

5.3.2 Avoidance of triple negation

Triple negation is also typically seen as incorrect in standard English because it causes unnecessary complexity and redundancy in a sentence. In standard usage, one negative is sufficient to convey the intended meaning.

> She *can't never* find *nothing* in her room.
> (→ She *can* never find *anything* in her room.)
> He *didn't* do *nothing* to *nobody*.
> (→ He didn't do *anything* to *anybody*.)
> I *don't* want *no* trouble with *nobody*.
> (→ I don't want *any* trouble with *anyone*.)

5.3.3 Correct double negation

In some cases, two negatives are employed to intensify or nuance the meaning rather than to cancel each other out. This usage is common in expressions that imply a mild or moderate degree of something, or in situations where the double negative highlights an inevitable or universally true fact.

> It was a not unpleasant surprise. ('a passably pleasant surprise')
> He didn't act unkindly. ('somewhat/moderately kindly')
> You can't not understand the importance of this.
> ('You cannot help understanding the importance of this.')
> I didn't find his explanation unhelpful.
> ('His explanation was somewhat helpful')
> There is no rule without exception. ('Every rule has exceptions.')

5.4 Adjectives and adverbs

5.4.1 Confusion between adjectives and adverbs

The confusion between adjectives and adverbs arises because both describe or modify other words, but they serve different roles in a sentence.

- Certain adjectives are informally used as adverbs in casual speech, as shown below:

  She runs *quick*. (informal, commonly used in casual speech)
  She runs *quickly*.
  He is a *real* good singer. (informal)
  He is a *really* good singer.
  He spoke *loud* at the meeting. (informal)
  Can you speak *louder*? I can't hear you. (informal)

- Adjectives are used after linking verbs and describe or characterize the subject, as illustrated below:
  *She *seems happily*. (→ She seems *happy*.)
  *He *feels badly* about the situation. (→ He feels *bad* about the situation.)
  *She *looks beautifully*. (→ She looks *beautiful*.)
  *He painted the fence *whitely*. (→ He painted the fence *white*.)

The above examples show common errors in which adjectives should be used after linking verbs instead of adverbs.

- Adverbs often indicate manners of action expressed by the verb, as shown in the examples below:

She sings *beautifully*/*beautiful.
He read the instructions *carefully*/*careful before assembling them.

- *Fast*, *early*, and *long* are examples of adjectives and adverbs that have the same form (known as **flat adverbs**), unlike most other words that typically add *-ly* to form an adverb. These words are used to modify verbs without any change in form, as shown in the examples below:

He arrived *early/*earlily* at the airport.
He drives *fast/*fastly*.
He stayed *long/*longly* at the party last night.

- Some adverbs, such as *high*, *hard*, *late*, and *pretty*, have the same form as their corresponding adjectives, while others add the suffix *-ly* to form the adverb. Additionally, certain adverbs like *high/highly*, *hard/hardly*, *late/lately*, and *pretty/prettily* have different meanings and uses depending on their form, as shown in the examples below:

She jumped *high* to catch the ball. (physical height)
They spoke *highly* of her performance at the conference. (high degree)
He dove *deep* into the water. (physical depth)
He was impressed deeply. (the degree or intensity of his impression)
He studied *hard* for the exam. (manner)
She *hardly* slept last night because of the noise. (‘barely or almost not’)
The flight arrived *late* at the airport. (‘after the arranged time’)
We haven’t seen him much *lately*. (‘recently’)
She sings *pretty* well for a beginner. (‘fairly, very’)
She danced *prettily* at the party, charming everyone. (‘beautifully’)

5.4.2 Comparison

1. Use of definite article before comparative

Unlike the construction *comparative form + than*, the definite article *the* normally occurs before the comparative form when it is followed by the *of the two* phrase, as the entity with the greater degree of the relevant quality out of the two compared entities is already specified or determined. The structure *the + comparative form of the two* is used to compare two entities based on a particular quality, with one showing a greater degree of that quality, as shown in the examples below:

Sarah is *the better* of the two artists.
Kate is *the more* experienced of the two chefs.
This book is *the more* interesting of the two novels.

2. Intensifiers with comparatives

Intensifiers for comparatives are words or phrases used to emphasize or strengthen the comparative form of an adjective or adverb, such as *much*, *a lot*, *a great deal*, *far*, *by far*, *still*, and *even*. The intensifier *very* is typically used with adjectives and adverbs, but it does not occur directly before comparative forms, as shown in the following:

Steve is *much/a lot/far/still/even/a great deal/*very* older than Sue.

3. Intensifiers with superlatives

There are also intensifiers for superlatives, such as *by far*, *ever*, *easily*, *absolutely*, *undoubtedly*, and *quite*.

Baseball and soccer are *by far* the most popular sports in Korea.
This is *by far* the best meal I've ever had.
This movie is *by far* the most exciting of the trilogy.
That is the greatest novel *ever*.
It was *easily* the most impressive performance I've seen.
It's *absolutely* the most exciting event of the year.
This is *undoubtedly* the most beautiful sunset I've ever seen.
It was *quite* the most impressive performance I've seen. (BE)

In these examples, superlative intensifiers like *by far*, *ever*, *easily*, *absolutely*, *undoubtedly*, and *quite* emphasize the extreme degree of the superlative. The sentence *It was quite the most impressive performance I've seen* is commonly used in British English.

4. Various superlative constructions

There are various ways to express superlative meanings, as illustrated in the examples below:

This painting is *the most* beautiful *of all* the artworks in the gallery.
This painting is *more* beautiful *than any other* artwork in the gallery.
This painting is *as* beautiful *as can be* in the gallery.
No other artwork in the gallery is *more* beautiful *than* this painting.
No other artwork in the gallery is *as* beautiful *as* this painting.

The definite article *the* is typically omitted when comparing multiple situations or instances of the same entity, as illustrated in the examples below:

She is *most productive* in the morning.
He feels *happiest* when he's with his family.

Spring is *mildest* in April.
She is *fastest* when she runs on the track.

5. Some comparative constructions from Latin

Some comparative constructions are derived from Latin loanwords, such as *superior to*, *inferior to*, *junior to*, *senior to*, *anterior to*, *posterior to*, *prior to*, and others. These phrases express comparative meanings, where one entity is evaluated in relation to another. For example, *superior to* means 'higher in rank, quality, or importance,' while *inferior to* indicates 'lower in rank or quality.' These constructions are commonly used in both formal and academic contexts to compare entities based on their attributes or status as follows:

Her knowledge of the subject is *superior to* mine.
The company's customer service is *inferior to* that of its competitors.
He's *junior to* his colleagues but very capable.
In the corporate hierarchy, she is *senior to* most of her colleagues.
The event is scheduled for a date *anterior to* the holiday break.
The meeting is planned *posterior to* the workshop.
The research team conducted an initial survey *prior to* the field study.

6. Other constructions

The sequence of comparative form and comparative form, such as *colder and colder* or *faster and faster*, is used to describe an increasing or intensifying quality over time. This structure emphasizes that something is becoming progressively more noticeable or prominent.

The wind grew *stronger and stronger*.

As the days passed, the weather became *colder and colder.*
The music grew *louder and louder* as the concert went on.
His explanations became *clearer and clearer* as he repeated them.
The day grew *hotter and hotter* as the afternoon went on.

5.5 Specific types of adverbial clauses

5.5.1 Absolute (participial) construction

An absolute clause is a non-finite or verbless clause that provides additional context to the main clause. It typically consists of a subject noun phrase and an optional participle (either in the *-ing* or *-ed* form), but it is not introduced by a subordinator (Greenbaum and Nelson 2016, Encyclopedia.com). This clause adds extra information, such as time, reason, or condition, and functions as an adverbial clause, providing supplementary details. Absolute clauses are often set off by commas.

The sun having set, we packed up our things and left the beach.
(= *After the sun had set*, we packed up …)
His homework completed, he went out to meet his friends.
(= *Because his homework was completed*, he …)
(= *After his homework had been completed*, he …)
The meeting over, everyone returned to their desks.
(= *Because the meeting was over, everyone ...*)
(= *After the meeting had been over*, everyone …)
Time permitting, we will finish the project tomorrow.
(= if/as long as time permits, ...)
Weather permitting, the event will be held outdoors.
(= if/as long as weather permits, ...)
All things considered, it was a successful event.

(= if all things are considered, ...)
The absolute clauses can indeed be converted to the full adverbial clauses in parentheses. The absolute clauses are reduced forms of the full adverbial clauses.

5.5.2 Dangling modifiers: unclear modifiers

A dangling modifier is a descriptive phrase or clause where its target of modification or association is uncertain or unknown, or its connection to the main clause is unclear. Specifically, its omitted subject does not match the subject of the main clause, which leads to a confusing sentence.

*While hiking up the mountain, the view was breathtaking.
(→ While hiking up the mountain, I was amazed by the breathtaking view.)
*Having finished her homework, the TV was turned on.
(→ Having finished her homework, she turned on the TV.)
*After finishing dinner, the dishes were cleaned.
(→ After finishing dinner, I cleaned the dishes.)
*While reading the book, the phone rang loudly.
(→ While reading the book, I heard the phone ring loudly.)
*While reading the book, Rachel phoned me.
(→ While reading the book, I got a call from Rachel.)
(→ While I was reading the book, Rachel phoned me.)

5.5.3 Adverbial participle (*-ing* or *-ed*) clauses

An adverbial participle clause is a non-finite clause that functions as an adverbial, modifying the main clause. It is formed using either the *-ing* form (present participle) or the *-ed* form (past participle) of a verb. These clauses provide additional information about the situation in the main clause, such as time, cause, condition, or concession. When the subject of an adverbial participle clause is the same as that of the main clause, the subject, along with a subordinator, is usually omitted to avoid repetition as follows:

Feeling exhausted, she went to bed early.
(= *Because she felt* exhausted, she went to bed early.)
Working hard all day, they finally finished the project.
(= *Because they worked* hard all day, they finally finished …)
Hearing the news, he couldn't believe it.
(= *When he heard* the news, he couldn't believe it. right?)
Being tired, he couldn't finish the project on time.
(= *Because he was* tired, he couldn't finish the project on time.)
Listening to music, I worked on my assignment.
(= *While I was listening* to music, I worked on my assignment.)
Walking through the park, she talked on the phone.
(= *While/When she was walking* through the park, she talked …)
Having enough time, we could go for a walk.
(= *Because we had* enough time, we could go for a walk.)
Feeling better, she will join us for dinner.
(= *If she feels* better, she will join us for dinner.)
Speaking slowly, he made sure everyone understood the situation.
(= *Because/As he spoke* slowly, he made sure everyone …)
Singing loudly, she captured everyone's attention.
(= *Because she sang* loudly, she captured everyone's attention.)
Having studied all night, she still didn't pass the exam.
(= *Although she had* studied all night, she still didn't pass the exam.)
Having trained for months, she still wasn't ready for the race.
(= *Though she had* trained for months, she still wasn't ready …)
Being tired, he couldn't finish the project on time.
(= *Because he was* tired, he couldn't finish the project on time.)

5.5.4 Impersonal absolute participial construction

An impersonal absolute participle is a specialized form of an absolute participial construction in which the subject, distinct from that of the main clause, is omitted or unspecified. It is a non-finite clause that provides additional context, background, or condition to the main clause, often conveying a general situation, condition, or circumstance under which the main action takes place.

Generally speaking, people tend to work harder when they are motivated.
Strictly speaking, this rule only applies to full-time employees.
Frankly speaking, I don't agree with your decision.
Putting it all together, the results were quite impressive.
Putting it mildly, the situation was a disaster.
Putting it into perspective, we had been working under extreme pressure.
Putting it bluntly, he didn't have the necessary skills.

5.6 Special constructions

Sentence-initial negative adverbs *hardly* and *scarcely* are followed by inversion, with the operator (*had*) preceding the subject, in the following constructions:

1. Hardly + had + S ... before/when S + V (past) ...

Hardly had I finished my breakfast *before* the doorbell rang.
Hardly had they boarded the plane *when* it started to rain heavily.
Hardly had he started his presentation *before* the projector malfunctioned.

Hardly had she stepped out the door *when* she realized she forgot her keys.

2. Scarcely + had + S ... before/when S + V (past) ...

Scarcely had the concert begun *when* the power went out.
Scarcely had I opened the book *when* my phone started ringing.
Scarcely had we started our vacation *before* we encountered a major delay.
Scarcely had they announced the winner *when* the crowd erupted in applause.
In the above examples, *hardly* and *scarcely* are placed at the beginning of the sentence to highlight the immediacy of the subsequent event. These sentences can be rephrased using the construction *as soon as + subject + verb (past)....*
As soon as I finished my breakfast, the doorbell rang.
As soon as the concert began, the power went out.

3. More inverted constructions

- Inversion refers to reversing the usual subject-verb order, often for emphasis or style. It is triggered by adverbs or phrases expressing negation or limitation, such as *never*, *seldom*, *not only*, etc. This structure adds emphasis, making sentences sound more formal or dramatic, and is commonly used in literature and formal writing to create an impact.

Not only did she forget her keys, but also she left her phone at home.
Not only have they repaired the roof, but they've also painted the walls.
Never have I seen such a beautiful sunset before.
Never will he forget the kindness she showed him.
Seldom have I seen such a beautiful performance.

Not a soul did he mention the surprise party to.
Not for a moment did they hesitate before making the decision.
Only after the meeting ended did we realize the importance of the discussion.
Only by working together can we achieve success.

- **Inversion triggered by place adverbs**: When place adverbs like *here* and *there* appear at the beginning of a sentence, they often trigger inversion with an intransitive verb and a non-pronominal subject. This structure emphasizes the action or event. Some examples are below:

Here comes the taxi.
Here is your cell phone.
There goes Tracy/the bus.
Here it is. Here/*There* he is. (The pronominal subject is not inverted.)

- **(Direction) adverb+verb (movement)+subject**: This construction places a directional adverb (e.g., *up*, *down*, *in*, *out*, *here*, *there*, etc.) at the beginning of the sentence, followed by an intransitive verb expressing movement (e.g., *come*, *go*, *run*, *walk*, etc.), and then the subject appears after the verb.

Out went the children to play.
Up went the price of gas.
There went the dog after the ball.

This construction emphasizes the movement or direction of an action, drawing attention to the path or arrival of something. It is more commonly found in written narratives, literature, or more formal contexts, rather than everyday conversation.

- The construction (place) adverb phrase + verb + subject places a location expression (such as *in the park*, *at the door*, *by the window*, etc.) at the beginning of the sentence, followed by the verb and subject. This structure emphasizes the location of the action or subject and is often used in narratives or descriptive writing to create vivid, descriptive scenes.

In the park played the children. (cf. In the park they played.)
On the hill stood an old castle.
By the window was a bird.

This fronting of the location element emphasizes and highlights the place, drawing attention to it. This is the result of the front focus principle, which places important or descriptive elements at the beginning to create a stronger impact.

Exercises

1. Choose the appropriate form of the verb from parentheses.

(1) Neither the cat nor the dogs (was/were) found in the yard.
(2) Every student in the class (has/have) completed their assignment.
(3) Either the teacher or the students (is/are) responsible for the project.
(4) The list of items (was/were) on the table.
(5) Each of the players (has/have) a unique skill set.
(6) The pair of shoes (look/looks) new.
(7) Each of the books (contain/contains) valuable information.
(8) The number of participants (has/have) increased significantly.
(9) A few of the cookies (was/were) left on the plate.
(10) A bouquet of flowers (bring/brings) joy to the room.

2. Complete the sentences with the correct relative pronoun.

(1) The teacher, _______ has years of teaching experience, explained the topic clearly.
(2) You can give the invitation to _______ you think will be interested.
(3) The scientist _______ discovery changed modern medicine won a prestigious award.
(4) He is the person to _______ you should send the email.
(5) The house _______ was built in the 1800s is now a museum.

3. Choose the appropriate form of the pronoun from the parentheses,

using a word preferred in more formal contexts if two options are possible.

(1) She was annoyed by (his/him) arriving late at the meeting.
(2) He regrets (me/my) decision to quit the team.
(3) She heard (them/their) arguing outside the pub.
(4) They were pleased with (their/them) contributing to the project.
(5) I look forward to (your/you) joining us for the event.
(6) She was worried about (his/him) forgetting the appointment.
(7) We are grateful for (their/them) helping us with the arrangements.
(8) The manager insisted on (his/him) providing the final report.
(9) They were disappointed with (their/them) not following the instructions.
(10) I admire (your/you) completing the task so quickly.

4. Choose the appropriate form of the verb from the parentheses, using a word preferred in more formal contexts.

(1) If I (be) you, I would reconsider that decision carefully.
(2) If you (have) (ask) for help, we could have finished the project much sooner.
(3) (Have) I (be) more aware of the risks, I would have made a different choice.
(4) I wish she (be) able to attend the meeting tomorrow.
(5) The lawyer recommended that his client (speak) with a financial advisor before making a decision.

Chapter 6

Information Packaging

Objectives

To understand various usages for information packaging, including:

- the front-focus and end-focus principles
- parenthetic expressions
- the end-weight principle
- avoidance of misplaced expressions
- parallelism in sentence structure
- avoidance of repeated words or sounds for clarity

Key words

front-focus principle, end-focus principle, parenthetic expressions; end-weight principle, avoidance of misplaced expressions, parallelism, avoidance of repeated words or sounds

Information packaging in grammar involves arranging sentence elements to highlight key details for clarity and emphasis, guiding the reader or listener through important points. This chapter examines how grammatical choices can help convey messages more effectively.

6.1 Emphasis

6.1.1 Front-focus principle

Front-focus is a process that places a specific part of a sentence at the beginning for emphasis, drawing attention to key details before introducing the rest of the sentence.

In the garden bloomed vibrant flowers.
Into the classroom walked the teacher.
Under the stars, we sat and talked for hours.
Gone are the days when we could rely on paper maps.
Pain relievers, Group A took, and *placebo pills*, Group B took.
Never did they expect such a warm welcome.
Only after the meeting did we realize the importance of the topic.

By fronting certain words or phrases, the writer draws attention to those elements, making them more prominent.

6.1.2 End-focus principle

End-focus is a principle that places the most important or new information at the end of a sentence. This helps emphasize key details and makes the message clearer by directing the reader's or listener's attention to the most significant part.

The team celebrated their victory *after a tough season.*
The presentation was a success, *thanks to her hard work.*
We will discuss the details of the plan *tomorrow.*
After months of hard work, they completed the project *on time.*

6.1.3 Parenthetic expressions

A parenthetic expression often serves to highlight or draw greater attention to the part of the sentence that comes before it.

The concert, to be honest, was not as good as I expected.
My brother, by the way, is an expert in artificial intelligence.
This issue, of course, needs further investigation.
Klimt's paintings, as a result, gained significant attention from art critics.

6.2 Comprehensibility

6.2.1 End-weight principle

The **end-weight principle** suggests that longer or more complex structures tend to be placed at the end of a sentence. This is done to make the sentence easier to process, as the more detailed or important information is typically saved for last.

The fact that the company has been cutting costs for years and still can't turn a profit is a major concern for investors. (awkward)
→ It is a major concern for investors that the company has been cutting costs for years and still can't turn a profit. (improved)
→ A major concern for investors is the fact that the company has been cutting costs for years and still can't turn a profit. (improved)
That the project was completed on time is very impressive. (awkward)
→ It is very impressive that the project was completed on time. (improved)
That she managed to solve the problem quickly is remarkable. (awkward)
→ It is remarkable that she managed to solve the problem quickly. (improved)
He gave his parents, brothers, and sisters some gifts. (awkward)
→ He gave some gifts to his parents, brothers, and sisters. (improved)

6.2.2 Misplaced expressions

Placing expressions in the wrong part of a sentence can confuse the meaning. Proper placement ensures clarity and comprehensibility by guiding the reader's attention to the most important part of the sentence.

a. They agreed to meet at the park *the next afternoon.*
b. *The next afternoon*, they agreed to meet at the park.
c. She decided to leave the city *the following morning.*
d. *The following morning*, she decided to leave the city.

The above pairs of sentences (a-b and c-d) illustrate semantic differences based on the position of the italicized phrases. These phrases modify the verbs they are closest to. In (a), for example, *the next afternoon* modifies *meet*, indicating when the meeting is planned to happen. In (b), *the next afternoon* modifies *agreed*, indicating when the decision to meet was made. In (c), *the following morning* modifies *leave*, indicating when she will leave. In (d), *the following morning* modifies *decided*, focusing on when she made the decision to leave.

Let us consider the following sentences:

She didn't understand how hard it had been for him *until she saw him in person.* (awkward)
→ *Until she saw him in person*, she didn't understand how hard it had been for her. (improved)
She explained that it was all a misunderstanding *calmly*. (awkward)
→ She explained *calmly* that it was all a misunderstanding. (improved)
→ She *calmly* explained that it was all a misunderstanding. (improved)

In each pair, the first sentence is awkward because the placement of the modifying phrases interrupts the flow of the sentence. This disrupts clarity and can make the sentence feel stilted. The second sentence, however, has the modifying phrase or adverbial clause placed more naturally, improving the clarity and flow. This corrected placement makes the sentence sound more natural and easier to follow.

6.2.3 Parallelism

Parallelism ensures consistency in sentence structure when presenting related ideas, making the sentence more organized, clearer, and easier to follow. It involves coordinating similar elements—such as noun phrases, verb phrases, or clauses—so that they match in form and maintain balance. Incorrect sentences are corrected below:

She enjoys *reading books*, *to watch movies*, and *playing games*.
→She enjoys *reading books*, *watching movies*, and *playing games*. (corrected)

The teacher asked us to *write an essay*, *complete the worksheet*, and *participating in the discussion*.
→The teacher asked us to *write an essay*, *complete the worksheet*, and *participate in the discussion*. (corrected)

He not only *finished his homework* but also *helping his sister with hers*.
→He not only *finished his homework* but also *helped his sister with hers*. (corrected)

The company values *innovation*, *collaborating*, and *customer satisfaction*.
→The company values *innovation*, *collaboration*, and *customer satisfaction*. (corrected)

She is *talented*, *hardworking*, and *is determined*.
→She is *talented*, *hardworking*, and *determined*. (corrected)

They postponed the meeting *because of the bad weather* and *they had scheduling conflicts.* (coordination of noun phrase and clause)

→They postponed the meeting *because the weather was bad* and *because they had scheduling conflicts.* (corrected: coordination of clauses)

→They postponed the meeting *because of the bad weather* and *the scheduling conflicts.* (corrected: coordination of noun phrases)

He couldn't attend the event *because of the heavy rain* and *that his car broke down.* (coordination of noun phrase and clause)

→He couldn't attend the event *because it rained heavily* and *his car broke down.* (corrected: coordination of clauses)

→He couldn't attend the event *because of the heavy rain* and *the car breakdown.* (corrected: coordination of noun phrases)

She was frustrated by *the long wait* and *there was loud noise at the concert.* (coordination of noun phrase and clause)

→She was frustrated by *the long wait* and *the loud noise at the concert.* (corrected: coordination of noun phrases)

Jane Campion won Academy Awards for *both screenwriting and for directing* for her two separate films, *The Piano* (1993) and *The Power of the Dog* (2021).

→Jane Campion won Academy Awards for *both screenwriting and directing* for her two separate films, *The Piano* (1993) and *The Power of the Dog* (2021). (corrected)

6.2.4 Avoidance of repeated words or sounds

It is better to avoid repeated words or sounds in order to enhance clarity and fluidity in writing. Here are some examples:

It's beginning raining.

→It's beginning to rain.

He enjoys playing tennis and playing basketball.

→He enjoys playing tennis and basketball.

At this *point*, I should *point out* that the experiment was successful.

→At this *point*, I should *mention* that the experiment was successful.

The main focus of my presentation is the impact of technology on education, and *the focus* is on its role in student engagement.

→*The main focus* of my presentation is the impact of technology on education and its role in student engagement.

The report describes how pollution affects the environment, and *the report* also explains its long-term consequences.

→*The report* describes how pollution affects the environment and explains its long-term consequences.

The book outlines the history of art movements, and *the book* also covers key artists and their contributions.

→*The book* outlines the history of art movements and covers key artists and their contributions.

The committee *will* evaluate the proposal and *will* assess its impact on the community.

→The committee *will* evaluate the proposal and assess its impact on the community.

Exercises

1. Rewrite the following sentences to correct the parallelism errors.

    (1) She enjoys reading books, swimming in the pool, and to walk in the park.
    (2) The meeting was long, boring, and it was difficult to stay awake.
    (3) I like to read books, watching movies, and playing video games.
    (4) The company values punctuality, good communication, and working well under pressure.
    (5) They are talented, creative, and they have a lot of ambition.
    (6) The teacher asked the students to read the chapter, to write a summary, and they must answer the questions.
    (7) The dog loves running in the park, jumping over obstacles, and to chase after the ball.

2. Rewrite the following sentences according to the end-weight principle.

    (1) To make decisions based on evidence rather than assumptions is necessary for good leadership.
    (2) Reading extensively on scientific advancements, taking notes on important theories, and synthesizing diverse viewpoints from multiple sources are crucial for writing a research paper.
    (3) That you have a balanced meal, exercise regularly, and get a good night's sleep is very important for your health.

References

문용. 2002. 고급영문법해설(2판). 서울: 박영사.

Aarts, Bas. 2011. *Oxford modern English grammar*. Oxford: Oxford University Press.

Akmajian, Adrian and Frank Henry. 1975. *An introduction to the principles of transformational syntax*. Cambridge, MA: MIT Press.

Azar, Betty Schrampfer. 1999. *Understanding and using English grammar*. NY: Pearson Education.

Cho, Nahmho. 2014. Five forms of English predicates and Adjuncts. *Studies in Linguistics* 33, 419-446.

Crystal, David. 2003. *The Cambridge encyclopedia of the English language* (2nd ed.). Cambridge: Cambridge University Press.

Denham, Kristin and Anne Lobeck. 2013. *Linguistics for everyone: An introduction*. Boston, MA: Cengage Learning.

Fillmore, Charles. 1968. The case for case. In Emmon Bach and Robert T. Harms, eds. 1968. *Universals in linguistic theory*, 1-90. New York: Holt, Rinehart, Winston.

Greenbaum, Sidney and Gerald Nelson. 2009. *An introduction to English grammar*. New York: Pearson Education.

Han, Hak-Sung. 2008. A study on the origin and adequacy of the notion of the five forms of the sentence in English grammar. *Journal of British & American Studies* 19, 153-182.

Hornby, Albert Sydney. 1975. *A guide to patterns and usage in English*. Oxford: Oxford University Press.

Huddleston, Rodney and Geoffrey K. Pullum. 2002. *The*

Cambridge grammar of the English language. Cambridge: Cambridge University Press.

Hwang, Kyu-Hong. 2016. An argument structure-based approach to sentence patterns in English. *New Korean Journal of English Language and Literature* 58(4), 233-253.

Jung, Duk-Kyo. 2010. A study on English sentence patterns and its application: English 5 verb patterns revisited. *Korean Journal of General Education* 4(2), 177-204.

Kearns, Kate. 2000. *Semantics*. London: Macmillan Press.

Kim, Sungwook. 2014. *English syntax: An introduction to generative theory*. Seoul: Shinasa.

Maugham, W. Somerset. 2005. *The moon and sixpence*. New York: Penguin Books.

Nam, Wahn. 2014. Sentence patterns of English. *Studies in Linguistics* 32, 101-124.

Nelson, Gerald and Sidney Greenbaum. 2016. *An introduction to English grammar*. New York: Routledge.

O'Conner, Patricia T. and Stewart Kellerman. 2009. *Origins of the specious: myths and misconceptions of the English language*. US: Random House Publishing Group.

O'Grady, William. 1998. *Syntax files*. ms.

Onions, Charles Talbut. 1904. *An advanced English syntax*. London: Kegan Paul, Trench, Trubner & Co. Ltd.

Palmer, Frank. 1990. *Modality and the English modals*. London: Longman.

Quirk, Randolph, Sidney Greenbaum, Geoffrey Leech, and Jan Svartvik. 1985. *A comprehensive grammar of the English language*. London: Longman.

Ross, John Robert. 1967. *Constraints on variables in syntax*. Doctoral dissertation, MIT.

Swan, Michael. 2005. *Practical English usage* (3rd ed.). Oxford: Oxford University Press.

Concise Oxford companion to the English language. *Encyclopedia.com.*
Cambridge Dictionary
Longman Dictionary of Contemporary English Online
Merriam-Webster Dictionary
Oxford English Dictionary
Oxford Learner's Dictionaries
The Free Dictionary

Index

E

F

G

H

I

M

박인규

충북대학교 영어영문학과 학사
성균관대학교 대학원 영어영문학과 석사
미국 하와이 주립대학교 언어학과 박사
현재 충북대학교 영어영문학과 교수

Understanding English Grammar

초판 1쇄 발행 _ 2025년 2월 28일

저　　자 • 박 인 규
발 행 인 • 정 현 걸
발　　행 • 신 아 사
인　　쇄 • 삼일문화
출판등록 • 1956년 1월 5일 (제9-52호)
주　　소 • 서울특별시 은평구 통일로 59길 4
전　　화 • 02)382-6411 · 팩스 02)382-6401
홈페이지 • www.shinasa.co.kr
E-MAIL • shinasa@daum.net

ISBN 979-11-7342-077-1 (93740)

정가 15,000원